Why Study

SOCIOLOGY ?

Why Study SOCIOLOGY?

Elliott Krause

Northeastern University

Random House   New York

First Edition

9 8 7 6 5 4 3 2 1

Library of Congress Cataloging in Publication Data

Krause, Elliott A
  Why study sociology?

  Includes bibliographical references and index.
  1. Sociology. I. Title.
HM51.K68   301   79-20938
ISBN 0-394-32200-2

Manufactured in the United States of America.

For Kim, Helen, Laddie, and Stripes

CONTENTS

PREFACE

Why study sociology? This book is based on the premise that this question is a legitimate one for a beginning student to ask. Often it is not asked, or answered, in introductory sociology courses. The professor assumes the value of learning sociology to be high. Naturally, since he or she is likely to be spending a lifetime working at it. And many texts start with a brief pep talk, then quickly turn to a formal discussion of theory and methods. Then the fields of sociology are introduced, one by one.

I've organized this little book differently, to answer the question posed in the title. From your point of view, as a student, what's in sociology for you? That question deserves a real answer, and the answer can be meaningful to you personally. Sociology can help you understand yourself and your relationships, your work life, your experiences in your community, and your political action or inertness. It can make you think more broadly about the social world we all live in. I hope to show you how all this is so.

My personal approach to you as the reader will require me to put myself on the line as well. I'll introduce myself and some of my experiences to you as we go along. There is a point of view, a philosophy, behind this way of writing that I hope will become clear as you read on. Sociologists are *people,* individuals who don't always agree with one another about the point of view the field is taking as a whole. I want to respect and present this fact in the book, not hide it. There is a good reason. Controversy and disagreement within the field are sometimes kept from beginning students. It is sometimes assumed that they would get confused. They are thought to be too naive to understand anything but a false "united front" style of sociology. Now some who support such suppression of controversy do so with the genuine desire to simplify now in order to present

ix

controversies later. But frequently "later" never comes, for students can and do vote with their feet. Their first course in sociology becomes their last.

I intend to respect your basic intelligence and common sense. Also, I know that it takes some doing and considerable social experience to get where you have already gotten in life. Controversy and disagreement will not be kept out of this first primer, or introduction to an introduction. Also, from my point of view—and I hope you will eventually agree with me—the *debates* within the field, debates over issues and interpretations of what's going on, are what give the field its life and interest. So in my argument for sociology I will stress its ability to involve you quickly in some of the key issues that are presently stirring up both the field and the wider society. This will mean more of a focus on problems than on theory, but theory will not be neglected. Some political and philosophical arguments that lie behind theory in sociology will be presented, along with some of the main ideas of the classic sociological thinkers, especially those of Karl Marx, Max Weber, and Emile Durkheim.

My personal approach is geographical as well. My corner of the world—north of Boston on the Merrimac River at the New Hampshire line, in a small town called Batesville—will be featured in this book. I'm not for a minute implying that you should be fascinated by where I live.

But it *is* where I live. Since I'm going to bring myself and my experiences into play in the book, the place where the action is going on will need to be described. Some sociology gets a little abstract, and bringing my home town into it and exploring that community sociologically will be good insurance against that danger. I love the South, especially the Mississippi delta country and New Orleans, and the Southwest, the big sky country, and the West Coast. But New England is where I live, and where I will set the stage for some of the book.

Another difference from some introductory sociology books will be the absence of the technical language of sociology—what students and some professors call "the jargon." I will define and discuss briefly some of the key concepts and terms of sociology as we go along. But my book will not present all the terms in sociology. Nor will it systematically introduce you to all the research areas of the field. These are jobs for a full textbook, or a complete course using a series of books and lectures.

This book, then, has been designed as a bridge between your everyday understanding of social life and the kind you can develop through the study of sociology. If you do not have a broad overview of all that sociology is doing, by the time you finish this book, I hope that you will have a strong sense of some of the ways that sociology can be relevant to your life. Think of this as the appetizer. Think of any full introductory sociology course you are taking as the main entree. Think of this as the *why*, the full course as the what.

A preface is the proper place to thank those who helped the author along the way. My greatest debt is to a small group of students in introductory sociology at Harvard Summer School in the summer of 1977. Together we read and discussed the first draft of each chapter. Their comments were critically important in my first revision. If they didn't find something we read useful, I felt there was no point in proceeding further with it. I'm also grateful to Al Helfeld, for his initial encouragement on the idea, I want to thank my editors at Random House, Barry Fetterolf and Phil Metcalfe, for their support and understanding. They helped me through the three years between the original idea and the final version. Thanks as well to the following sociologists whose helpful comments and criticisms have helped to make this work more accurate and relevant to the rather unusual purpose I had in mind: Norman Goodman, William Snizek, Dean Eastman, and Arnie Arluke. I would also like to thank my family. My children, Carol and Andy, and my wife Thea, were understanding as I paced the floor and agonized, page by page. The four to whom this book is dedicated were a source of warm and steady encouragement.

E.K.
March 1979

Why Study
SOCIOLOGY ?

INTRODUCTION
Why Study Anything?

One of the most gifted of teachers, the great classical scholar Gilbert Highet, spent a lifetime wondering about the gap between his own excitement in studying and learning and the attitude he found in many people. He asked:

> Why is teaching so difficult for the teachers? And why is learning nearly alway so hard for the pupils? There are many reasons; but one certainly is that, as most schools are set up in the Western world, learning is something *compulsory* ...[1]

This being compulsory, being required, has consequences for how learning feels:

> Too often, for too many of us, learning appears to be an imposition, a surrender of our own will power to external direction, indeed a sort of enslavement. This is a mistake. On the contrary, learning is a natural pleasure. It is a pleasure inborn and instinctive, one of the earliest pleasures and one of the essential pleasures of the human race.[2]

Highet went on to note that a teacher must care about the subject being taught, must be enthusiastic and want to talk about it to others. I care about sociology. I think that it is one of the most interesting fields a person can spend a working lifetime in. I also think it is an important source of ideas and information that may help to make our

1

society a better one. And my job in this book is to get you to see the field somewhat as I do. It is to get you to want to go on reading in it long after any sociology course you take is over, to get you to pick the sociology books off the shelf at the neighborhood bookstore years after you have finished your formal education. It is also to get you to use what you have learned to change your ideas about yourself and your relations with others, about your work, about your community and about acting politically. Each of these will be a chapter. But before I introduce the book, let me introduce myself.

I'm Elliott Krause, a sociology professor at a large urban university in Boston—Northeastern University. I was born in the midwest, but since my father was stationed in South Carolina during World War II, I went to elementary school in Columbia, South Carolina. We returned to Ohio, where I went to junior high and high school. Then I went east to college, to Harvard. I loved the Boston area and went to grad school there, and then stayed on. My wife and our two children, plus our dog and two cats and goldfish and the rabbit, live today in Batesville, in an old (1740) colonial house that we helped restore, on the banks of the Merrimac River near Newburyport, Massachusetts, about an hour north of Boston and about four miles in from the sea. I like to cook (Italian and French primarily), play tennis and ski. Though I primarily write and do research in political sociology and the sociology of health care, I occasionally teach "intro" to students. Three summers ago I hit on the idea of a book that would try to explain to students or to anyone who might pick it up why I like the field. I decided to write it as I teach it, attempting to produce converts who share my enthusiasm and interest.

People have been looking over their back fence at their neighbors and finding it interesting for a long time, but our modern way of looking at social life in general evolved very slowly. The story of how this happened will bear reviewing here. We'll consider the transition from a time when thinking sociologically was nearly impossible to a time when events began to suggest it as a natural development. Then two founders of sociology, Auguste Comte and Karl Marx, will be presented to show the way in which sociologists began to disagree, even at the birth of their field, on what it was and what should be done with it. We will then take up two key questions: What do sociologists study? And how do they study it?

Inventing Sociology

For us, time flows like a river, in a direction. Look at the celebrations on New Year's Eve, the magic moment when one year turns into the next. A *new* year suggests progress, change, leaving the past behind. But there was a time in the history of Western civilization, now called the Middle Ages, when time was a never-changing cycle, the natural cycle of the seasons—fall, winter, spring, summer, back to fall. People lived close to the land-most as peasants. In those days the church stood above all men, as the representative of God on earth, and kings ruled "by the Grace of God." What this meant in practice was that no one could have legitimate power unless the church said it was legitimate. The Pope or his representative crowned the king. Then if the king were to disobey God's laws, as the church interpreted them, he could be excommunicated, lose his right to rule, and immediately become fair game for assassination.

The official view of the social order was hierarchical, with God at the top, the Pope directly below, then the king, followed by the nobles, followed by the serfs and peasants. And people were told by the church to accept the fact that they were born into, and would according to the Bible, "remain in that calling to which they had been called by God."³ Anyone who disagreed with this would be challenging not only the right of the kings and nobles to be where they were but also the right of the church to say that the hierarchical order should *stay* the way it was.⁴ Not that there weren't occasional peasant uprisings. In some eras the church and kings ganged up on the nobility. Other allegiances were set up from century to century to humble arrogant kings or remove troublesome Popes. But in general, to want what we now call social mobility, a better life than the one you were born into, or even to publicly go around suggesting that you looked at things differently from the church and the king—that was likely to get you hanged. You could be hanged on two grounds: disobeying the church, for which a church court would condemn you to burn in hell, and preaching revolution, for which the king's or noble's court would dispatch you to the afterlife the church said you were going to have. *Belief* in this order held it all together, as to this day it holds any totalitarian state together, and makes people like sociologists—the observers and talkers and questioners—the enemy. New ideas in any area, such as science or a new social order, were strongly discouraged. Along the way the people were often badly oppressed by their secular rulers, who often also worked hand in glove with the church to keep things in line, and to keep power and wealth in the hands of a few.

But people have a way of inventing things that aren't supposed to exist, including social arrangements prohibited by the ruling ideology of the time. For example, at the local level, in the small feudal villages, and especially in England, people acted much of the time as if the church were not really there. A "local political control" idea grew slowly out of the feudal era.[5] And gradually, as the centuries passed, the Middle Ages waned, and a new technological order grew. Communication improved. The cities grew, and modern international commerce was born, along with the particular form of economic and social arrangement we now call capitalism. These changes in the world of work and politics led to a new way of looking at things. Change, growth, riches, and their pursuit began to take over people's minds.

The social world was changed irrevocably by this rise of commerce. It had a particular economic form. Beginning in the late 1700's, we call it *industrial capitalism*—the centralizing of work in buildings where the owner bought the time and labor from the worker, in larger and larger settings, piling up and reinvesting the profits every year. Under industrial capitalism more and more people went to work for low wages in the growing factories, under worse and worse social and environmental conditions. New nation-states, formed at the end of the Middle Ages, grew at first because the overall authority of the Church had begun to wane; they formed the home for the new capitalism. However, just as soon as capitalists came to power in each of these nations, the next stage grew inevitably-capitalism began to spread across the boundaries of the nations. The changes were rapid. Marx and his collaborator, Friedrich Engels, summed it up this way. Capitalism

has drawn from under the feet of industry the national ground on which it stood. All old-established national industries have been destroyed or are daily being destroyed. They are dislodged by new industries whose introduction becomes a life and death question for all civilized nations, by industries that no longer work up indigenous raw material, but raw material drawn from the remotest zones; industries whose products are consumed, not only at home, but in every corner of the globe.[6]

But I am getting ahead of our story. For earlier, during the late 1600's and early 1700's, at the onset of the new social era, a special time developed that was to have important consequences for the history of sociology. This was a time when many learned people turned a new light of reason directly on society. They began to treat it as they were treating the physical world, without the blinders of the dogma of the medieval church.

The Enlightenment: Classics and a Wild Boy

In the new period, the European social elite, the only ones who could read, now looked at the natural world as a thing to be studied. They found that looking anew at the physical world soon led to looking in a new way at the social world as well. The classic writings of the Greeks and Romans, who managed without a God and a Pope, were rediscovered. The questions about the best, the ideal society, that Plato, Socrates, and a whole range of Roman political thinkers asked, began to be asked again. What people were thinking about these matters, they soon began to write down. Most importantly, they began to ask general, almost abstract questions about the way the society they lived in functioned. Then they began to contrast this with a model of society that implied a new way of arranging things socially, a new social order. To do this meant to describe the bits and pieces of the new social order and to invent terms and ideas to describe any society. And people began to think about the old social hierarchy that was dissolving around them. If it was not to last forever, what should a new order look like? What was possible? Immanuel Kant, the German philosopher, called this new rise of social thought "The Enlightenment," or in German, *die Aufklarung*, or clearing up—the sun coming out after the storm and darkness.[7]

This time period which most scholars date from the early eighteenth century to about the last decade of that century, was a great time for social philosophy—for discussions about the ideal society, the possible society, the future society. And we have much evidence that the Greek and Roman writings about the ideal political order, rediscovered in this period by French and English thinkers, were precisely what Thomas Jefferson, Alexander Hamilton, Benjamin Franklin, and others used for ideals and models for the United States Constitution, which was designed between 1776 and 1789.[8] These thinkers were not sociologists in the modern sense, but they were way ahead of their time as political analysts, and there is no question that the social philosophers of the time were a strong influence on these founding fathers. Just to look at the books on the shelf at Monticello, Jefferson's home, is to confirm this. I have, and I saw many old friends from the social thought of this time in Europe. And these Americans were able to form a governmental arrangement that still exists more than two centuries later, though it has been much modified.

One of the big debates of the time was over the issue of what kind of society could be built if you took men and women as the building blocks. Three thinkers took three points of view that to this day raise issues that are still studied, for they are still problems to us. The first was Thomas Hobbes. Observing the bloody record of history and the bloody revolution in England at the time he was writing, he suggested that a strong ruler and a strong system of discipline and order were necessary to hold people in line, since most of them were illiterate, greedy, aggressive, and stupid. He was much in favor of what we nowadays call an authoritarian state. The front illustration of his major work, *Leviathan*, shows a picture of a man (society) with a head labeled "king," arms labeled "nobility," and legs and feet labeled "peasantry."[9] Would you ask the feet of society to give the directions and do the thinking?

In the middle of the road in this debate stood John Locke. He felt that though men could be unreasonable in the short run (no one wrote seriously about women, though their real role was quite important), they could also reasonably agree as individuals to abide by a set of sensible rules and share a set of noes. This set of agreements he called[10] "the social contract." It was very similar to what sociologists would later describe as shared norms and values. This social contract was not written down but it operated, and it did not need Hobbes' Leviathan state to hold everyone in line.

On this issue Jean-Jacques Rousseau stood at the opposite pole from Hobbes. He had a theory of the purity and goodness of people before they are ruined by the bloody society and history described by Hobbes, before they are taught greed, hate, cruelty, and love of power. Human nature was basically good, said Rousseau; it was the existing social arrangements that taught people their bad habits, that set them against one another, that suppressed their abilities and turned them bitter and hostile. So, optimistically, all we need to do is to change the existing social arrangements into a form that would allow the good in people to come out while eliminating the need for the bad. No specific suggestions were given as the precise shape of this new society, but Rousseau suggested, reasonably, that people start looking around the world at the arrangements a lot of non-Western societies had come up with.[11]

Two things need saying at this point. First, the above is a great oversimplification of a much more complicated debate on the part of all three of these thinkers. Each had a whole realm of thought on the subject, which I have simplified here in order to make a point about assumptions and the nature of the theory that follows from them: the less you think people are capable of, the stricter the government you propose for them. Second, the debate does indicate that people were beginning to wonder what was basic to the biological creature Homo sapiens and what was the product of "society", whatever that was. If you were with Hobbes, you would be likely to want a strong, possibly dictatorial state to hold the basically awful people in line. But if you were with Rousseau, you would probably want a revolution *against* such an arrangement and the creation of a minimally restricting social environment that would not ruin basically good people or set them against one another. Thinkers were edging ever closer to a deliberate, conscious model of society. They had not quite left the old tradition which preached about the desirable society, and had not thought of direct research and description to create a theory of what society really was. But they were moving strongly in this direction.

One of the things the new social investigators looked for was a natural experiment. What if they were to find a wild child, one who had not grown up in society? Would this child be evil and unsocialized, savage, in need of Hobbes-style remedies? Or would the child be unspoiled and naïve, generous, loving, and kind, á la Rousseau? In 1797, in the woods near Aveyron, France, a wild child was sighted. He was occasionally seen and chased for almost two years. Finally he was caught and then brought to an early French psychologist, Itard, in January 1800.[12] Naturally, the thinkers of the time were excited, and debates about what the child would be like went on for months in the newspapers and scientific journals of Paris.

Itard found the boy slow in responding, unable to talk, and probably handicapped in other ways, such as being almost completely deaf. In a touching tribute to his own belief in the reclaimability and rehabilitation potential of handicapped people, Itard took over, almost full time, the attempt to socialize the boy and to teach him sign language. It was a long and heartbreaking task, and it mainly failed. Esquiriol, a famous and, like Itard, progressive psychologist of the time, summed up the effort and what it really may have meant as an experiment in rehabilitating a society-less child:

> The issue is debated; the best methods, the most enlightened care are brought to bear for the education of the so-called savage; but from all these claims, from all these efforts, from all these assurances, from all these hopes, what is the result? That the doctor has judged rightly; the alleged savage was nothing other than an idiot. Let us conclude from all this that men utterly without intelligence, found isolated in the mountains, in the forest, are imbeciles, idiots lost or abandoned.[13]

Modern analysts, such as Harlan Lane, believe that wild boy of Aveyron had every strike against him. He was probably retarded, and in addition he may well have been abandoned at the time of the critical years of language learning, which we now know must go on in the presence of others—in society, that is—or the child will never catch up.

The study of the wild boy solved nothing, but it did point up the importance of society to human beings. What was absent was a sociological theory, or model, of just what society was, or what it did for people. What was also missing was a theory of *socialization*, of the process by which the newborn is brought up to become the adult member of society. But soon two models of society were built—and they and their authors disagreed with one another.

Comte Versus Marx: An Argument Between Two of the Founders

Comte and Marx were the builders of systematic models of society, in the last half of the nineteenth century. They were large-scale theories on the nature of society, and there were explicitly *called* theories by these two founders of sociology. One, Comte, invented the term "sociology" for the new field of the study of society. Each of these two theories was soon to have readers, followers, and researchers testing out the validity of what it had to say, and we could genuinely say that sociology had begun to exist in its modern sense. Yet the debate these men created lasts to the present day, for it is a debate not only over what sociology should study but also over what should be done with the results.

Auguste Comte was an engineering student at France's elite government-run school, the École Polytechnique, in the early 1800s. He became involved in a student strike against the old-fashioned methods of the school, then dropped out in disgust over them and became a pupil of the brilliant social philosopher Henri Saint-Simon. Saint-Simon had dreams of reforming France which began to rub off on his pupil; these same ideas influenced Marx a number of years later.

Comte eventually went his own way, lived as a poor tutor in a garret in Paris, and wrote. In his first great volume he announced that a new science of society called sociology should be built, to help understand what it was that kept the social order the same and what factors made it change. Lewis Coser, in a book on social theorists, notes the special message of this first work:

> Comte's aim was to create a naturalistic science of society, which would both explain the past development of mankind and predict its future course. . . . The society of man, Comte taught, must be studied in the same scientific manner as the world of nature. It is subject to basic laws, just as is the rest of the cosmos, even though it presents added complexities.[14]

Comte thought that observing society, comparing societies, and, finally, looking at the development of societies historically would lead to the discovery of the "laws of motion" and the "laws of stability" that worked for all societies. He was no modest scholar. With the passing of the years he came to feel that his extremely oversimplified version of social evolution—all societies were supposed to go through the same three stages from primitive to modern —was enough. He not only had developed the first theory but also thought that no more were necessary.

But people kept on fighting one another, and eventually Comte decided that just theory was not enough. Now he wanted sociologists to advise the powerful new industrialist class, and he wanted them to uplift everyone morally in order to make sure that society's needs were taken care of as well as those of individuals. No one listened.

His next, more desperate idea was a sociological "Church," with robes and services where one would learn to be moral and socially responsible. He wanted all to get converted, especially the industrialists, who he accurately foresaw would be the ones running the society. He wanted the sociologists to be advisors to the men of power, the Kissingers advising the Prince. He did not believe in equal wealth for all, or sharing power, or democracy. We could in many ways consider him the first technocrat or social planner. This founder of sociology wanted it to become a set of skills and information to help those in power do their job more effectively, but not a force to rock the boat.

Karl Marx, born in 1818, about twenty years after Comte, could not have disagreed more with this goal. Marx went to a German university and received his Ph. D. in economics, then soon got involved in radical politics. In the repressive Germany of his time, that made him unemployable. So he moved to Paris, where he earned his living for a while as, of all things, the European commentator for the New York *Tribune*. Marx's theory was to live on into the present in a direct way. It was not to become the curiosity that Comte's soon became. Marx went through many stages of thinking and theory development, and never thought he had all the answers. Almost from the start of his work, Marx shared some of Comte's idealism and wish to change society. Though he shared with Comte the goal of a theory that would cover almost all social forces-the big picture—he had many differences with Comte both about what a theory was and what one should do with it. Marx was *not* interested in building an academic or intellectual empire to be called "sociology." He was a theorist interested in combining into one model the economic factors, political factors, and social-group factors involved in the creation of social change. And he did far more than write or preach. He studied specific historical periods with great care, to see how the real complexities worked out in the long run.[15]

In his major theoretical work, *Capital*, Marx showed how change in technology led to the rise in power of the owners of the new kind of technology and the fall of the owners of the older kind. For example, in an agricultural age most power was in the hands of those who owned the land. But the change to an industrial era meant the rise in wealth and power of the new factory-owning class. The ones in each age who did not own the places where goods were made were always the powerless and would remain so until a new age when all the poor and the workers got together to "seize ownership and control of the means of production for themselves."[16] This was an analysis that was also a plan for action. After working it out in economic theory, he tried to get it going in reality. Increasingly, he had the support, funds, and companionship of Friedrich Engels, an English industrialist with a strong conscience. The two worked out the implications for action in all sorts of areas, including the reform of family life and a plan to end the exploitation of women. Mainly they tried to help the new working class of Europe, formed in the factories of each nation, get their own political movement started. Though he died almost penniless, Marx was respected by a small circle of activists and scholars that has grown steadily to this day. He said, "I am not a Marxist"— meaning that he thought of his work as hypotheses to be tested and if wrong to be corrected, not as some kind of unchallengeable truth. He spent twenty years doing daily research in the British Museum library to build his theory. He did not believe that the action he wanted could be based on emotions and riots; it had to be based on a tested theory of social change—his, of course.

Marx often wrote on the impossibility, if one really wanted to understand what was going on, of marking off clearly bounded areas for separate groups to study and calling them "economics," "political science," and "sociology." For the world does not have such distinct areas in it, especially if change in the world is what one is trying to understand. Marx also wrote at length on the reasons why people had to change their own minds about the rightness or the desirability of a situation—to change their "consciousness"—before any real and permanent political action could occur.[16] Economic trends could set things up for a change, but people still had to act, and before they did, they had to have a reason. So in a sense psychology was a part of Marx's thinking as well as the other areas. He also was quite explicit about how one went about testing a theory—not just with data, but with action. He furthermore stated that sociology or economics that refused to challenge the status quo, that refused to take on the powerful and ask embarrassing questions, was really part of the problem, part of the propaganda that a ruling group used to keep people down. No real neutrality was possible for a sociologist because avoiding issues meant not challenging them.[17]

In our time, almost a century after the main period in which Marx did most of his important theoretical work, some researchers have taken his ideas and modified them into testable sets of modern social theories, but others have turned some of these original ideas into a kind of religion without a God. In some socialist states, especially in the Soviet Union, the particular version of Marxian theory rewritten by Lenin is an official dogma, Marxism-Leninism, which cannot be tampered with by anyone under pain of imprisonment.[18] We, however, will be concerned in this book, not with dogma, but only with Marxian ideas as they help in criticizing our own present society, and as they help to break down the barriers between fields and add to our overall understanding of our social situation.

Comte and Marx represent two ways in which social thought has been used and can be used: to aid in the systematic development of an existing society, especially by way of consulting to its power centers in industry and government, and as a tool for analysis to radically transform it. Some present-day sociologists work rather extensively as consultants to government and industry—Comte's program. Others use Marxian ideas and critiques to work for long-run change in our institutions. Sociology is a wide field, wide enough to encompass both styles of work. Sometimes one person can be involved in both styles of work—for various reasons, such as a need to help pay the rent. As I have sometimes told myself, being one of these divided sociologists, it gets difficult at times to state just exactly where you stand!

What Do Sociologists Study?

A famous astronomer at a well-known college once gave his students a terrible jolt on a final exam. Expecting a long examination form, they were surprised to find the exam had been printed on a set of 3-by-5 index cards, one for each student. One sentence was on the card. It said, "Describe the universe and give two examples." The astronomer was joking, of course, but a sociologist could not easily pull this joke off. For sociology has as its subject matter everything that's social, that's not exclusively individual, and also the relations between personal factors—your mood, for example, or the color of your hair or your sex—and social factors closely intertwined with them. If this isn't a field that has the universe as its subject matter, it comes close. Obviously, most sociologists will specialize in some field or other, but they all have their eye on *society,* which I personally define as the broad pattern of relations between people, including all the attitudes, rules, and values that they share.

One of the first sociologists to try and pin down what it was that he was trying to understand was Emile Durkheim, a student of Comte's ideas, one of the last "founding fathers" of the field, and one of the first modern researchers, in such areas as the causes of suicide. He worked in the late 1800's and the first two decades of this century. Durkheim had trouble pinning down his subject-society. And if *he* had trouble, you should not expect that you will be able to pin our subject down that quickly either. Steven Lukes, a biographer of Durkheim who is himself a sociologist, shows how Durkheim edged around the problem of defining just what this entity "society" was. Here Lukes tells of some of the stabs Durkheim took at the problem:

> By 'society' he sometimes meant the social or cultural transmission of beliefs and practices ("a reality from which everything that matters to us flows"), sometimes the existence of association (for instance, "Society . . . is nothing other than individuals assembled and organized."), sometimes the imposition of socially prescribed obligations ("Society . . . is a great moral power"), sometimes the object of thought, sentiment and action ("society constitutes an end that surpasses us and at the same time appears to us as good and desirable") and sometimes just simply a real, concrete society—though even here he was ambiguous, using the term sometimes to mean society (France, for example) and sometimes particular groups and institutions within it (the State, the family, etc.).[19]

Of course we can answer to all of this, Why yes! society is all of those things, as well as some not so nice ones that Durkheim avoided mentioning. But in fact what you are specifically interested in will determine at least in part the way you view society and what it does and is. Using the old story about an elephant being felt and described by a group of blindfolded people, at one moment Durkheim is feeling the trunk ("society is a long, flexible, conical thing"), the next minute the tail ("society is a long rope with a brush on the end"), and so on.

I will not solve your definition problem for you. Your development of your own definition of society will come out of your studies and thought. But one thing can be said by way of introduction. Some sociologists study the *micro*, or small, picture—a set of relationships, the behavior of a group, a particular profession—while others study the *macro*, or big, picture—the whole society, or the world of international relations. This is the *size of the frame*. Some of us are microsociologists, and others of us macrosociologists in style and approach. Some of us in fact both in alternation—micro on Monday and macro in March, as it were. And in addition the trick of relating the specific micro issue to the big, society-wide picture is an essential element of many sociological studies. We try to some extent "to see the world in a grain of sand;" we also strive not to miss the forest by only looking at the trees.

The Scope of Sociology

This problem of deciding on the subject matter of sociology is very important because of the consequences this decision has for the uses that sociologists, and anyone, will ultimately make of its findings. Durkheim was pushing for a new, narrow, and special field. He was trying to stake out a special territory that could not be claimed by the economists, the political scientists, and the historians. And once he had rejected history, politics, economics, and psychology, he took what was left—the structure of human relationships—and said, "My field, not yours." Part of the argument Durkheim had with other academic fields has to do with how events are explained. Durkheim emphatically didn't think social happenings could be explained only in psychological terms—for example, that the rise of Nazism in Germany could be explained by statements about Hitler's childhood and certain personal characteristics of some Germans. How many others had hard times, and didn't cause the rise of a political movement?

On the other hand, part of Durkheim's reason for setting up his sociology as he did was related to the academic politics of the French university system. And still today, academic sociology departments battle with other departments over topic material and "turf" to keep up enrollments and the number of students majoring in the field. This battling, of course, often gets in the way of innovating, of thinking across boundaries, and of making real advances in knowledge.

Sociologists were not alone in battling over boundaries however, during those early years. The turn of the century was the time when almost all fields developed their present boundaries, with all kinds of casualties. For example, as economics became a professional field at the turn of the century, the narrow definition of economics—studying dollars and not the power relations between economic forces and social groups—led to some real persecution of reformer economists. Some, such as Lester Ward, were driven out of their jobs in academic economics departments into (shudder) sociology; one was driven out of his presidency of the American Economic Association.[20]

This need to have a clear subject, a laid-out field, is normal and natural, since a science cannot grow until it begins to pile up more than one study on a topic, and until at least a few people get together and decide to take up a set of related and defined problems. On the other hand, a sociology with blinders on managed, for example, to study the family for almost fifty years without getting into the power relations between husbands and wives and the sexist nature of most marriage arrangements. Then finally, in the 1960s, political forces, along with economic pressures, demanded a change. Sociologists had to take a wider look at the problem, refine the sociological concept of the family, and relate sociology to social action on the matter.

So, too, for sociologists' discussions about power. Until the sixties they were rather conservative in tone. The sixties was the great decade for the reintroduction of the old, classical, broad historical viewpoint, for relating social issues to the world of money and power. Many of the younger sociologists (and some just young in heart) who brought this viewpoint back were interested in making sociology more involved in local and national problems. Not surprisingly, then, they were also interested in breaking down the intellectual barriers between history and economics, sociology and psychology, sociology and history. They figured that this approach would be a more effective way to attack these problems. The world didn't have neatly bounded areas on it labeled "sociology," "history," and "economics," and issues often had (and have) the ability to cross over the boundary lines that academia puts up. Their critical approach often involved looking across these boundaries as Marx had done, at economics, history, sociology, politics, and the psychology of political action. Happenings of the late sixties and early seventies such as Vietnam and Watergate, also had their effect.

Today, I am happy to say, there seems to be more general and mutual acceptance between the two camps with their opposed viewpoints of what sociology should be and do—between the narrow specialists and the broad-scale social critics. It was a long time coming. And some of my colleagues in sociology may think I'm being too optimistic, even today. But much of the recent critical work tends to be both a little more careful than some of the propagandistic work of the sixties and still a lot more critical of the status quo than the dull and often sexist sociology of the decades from 1900 to 1950. Of course, there were always individual sociologists who were years ahead of their time. One such was C. Wright Mills, who wrote highly critically about the "military-industrial complex" in the late fifties. He pushed for a critical sociology and was ignored by the sociological establishment but read by millions. His work is still in print, and in many languages.

Some Styles of Work

One way to get to know people is to ask about their work. Not simply "What do you do?" for that is often a status game. Rather, "Why do you do your work the *way* you do it?" and "How do you feel about it?" Studs Terkel, a distinguished student of work, often asked this kind of question of the workers he met, as he interviewed them. If we only go so far as to ask sociological researchers what style of research, what kind of approach they use, we can begin to get some sense of the variety of activities that come under the name of the field.[21]

There are many. For a start, we can consider the historical approach, the survey-research approach, the community study, participant-observation strategy, mathematical modeling, the experimental approach, and artistry. There are still other ways of doing sociology, and most sociologists in fact use a combination of approaches. In addition, almost all are serious library scholars as well, digging up articles and books on their topic and related ones.

Appropriately, the *historical* approach has a long history of use in sociology. As we've seen, both Comte and Marx were historical scholars. Only with a sense of some point in the past from which a line runs to some point in the present can we draw the line further on and get the feel for the way the society is likely to be tomorrow. Max Weber, the great classical sociologist of bureaucracy, religion, and politics, mastered the history of his subject in seven languages.

Today, we still occasionally find broad-scale historical studies in this tradition. We also find research which looks at a typically sociological problem in a past era and then uses a combination of sociological and historical techniques to find out the social process of the time. An example would be Stephan Thernstrom's study of New-buryport, Massachusetts, the one-time clipper-ship port that I live near, which turned to industry in the nineteenth century.[22] He wanted to find out whether "getting ahead," improving one's social-class position, was easier then than it is today. I will discuss his study and what its results signify for us today in Chapter 3. The historical approach adds depth and in a sense creates social roots, whatever the sociological topic of interest.

Sociologists do *survey research* to get a sense of what a large sample of people, a cross-section, think about an issue. Just about any kind of question can be approached in this manner, but some are a lot easier to handle than others. The art and science of polling at election time was originally developed by sociologists. As students or as re-searchers, may sociologists have the experience of thinking through a problem to design a study and thinking of a set of questions to ask that follow from the overall design. Then they pick a sample of people whose answers to these questions will be truly relevant and go ahead and do the study. Usually the answers are coded on IBM cards for computer processing, though you can do a lot of your processing yourself, if your sample isn't too big, and feel a lot closer to things. Today there are even survey-research firms, such as the National Opinion Research Center or the Research Triangle Institute, that can be hired to do your surveys for you. But some sociologists, including me, tend to get a little edgy about the distance this puts between us and the data.

The *community study* is an approach that sociologists share with anthropologists and political scientists, though each group has differ-ent emphases and problems. Sometimes studies involve teams with all these specialties represented. Using the community as a natural unit for analysis, the research team tries to get a feel for the social whole. One can, for example, inspect a set of problems in a commu-nity, such as problems of mental health in a typical suburb. One can look at patterns of relationship, such as next-door-neighbor friendli-ness in an executive neighborhood or a working-class suburb. One can look at a particular ethnic subcommunity within a larger city, such as an Italian neighborhood in Boston or a black ghetto of Wash-ington, D.C. One can ask questions about just what a community *is*, anyway. For example, is it the sense of being together? The ability to watch out for one another? Community studies use a mix of research approaches but share a goal—to understand life in the size of social unit that is the largest one most of us can easily comprehend —the city or town or other community unit in which we live.

Participant observation involves jumping with both feet into social life as a participant, but usually in a role pretty much on the sidelines. Then one observes what is going on and develops an idea of what is important—basic and new—in the social process. One looks for what is symbolic and meaningful to the people themselves. Erving Goffman, for instance, took a job as a recreational aide in a large public mental hospital on the outskirts of Washington, D.C. He took notes, wrote them up, and created a file of observations that he later turned into an analysis of life inside the walls of any round-the-clock institution. *Asylums,* his work on the subject, is now a classic used by people who run many kinds of institutions to get an idea of what life is like to the inmates.[23] Another example: Julius Roth, sick with tuberculosis, sat in bed taking field notes on the passage of time and on staff-patient relations in the TB hospital.[24] He was cured of TB but not of the sociological habit! His book *Timetables* records the results of the experience. One of the great strengths of this style of research is the way it allows the reader to live the life lived by the researcher, to gain insight into worlds of social life otherwise barred and unreachable.

Mathematical modelers try to take the regular features of social life and make mathematical models of them which will artificially stand for real activities. If the model works, one can "operate on it," change some of the factors, and new results will come out that will suggest the changes that might happen in the real world if such factors were changed "out there" in society. Computers that translate from one language to another use a mathematical model of languages and of sentence-making behavior. Another kind of math model is used for those election-night computer projections of voting behavior with one-tenth of 1 percent of the sample in. It is a model of how all the other districts vote if the "special" precincts vote as they do. Situations of choice and chains of openings left below in an organization when someone gets promoted are other areas where math models are being developed. Though the math sometimes gets a bit complicated, the idea is a fairly simple one.

The *experimental approach* is often shared by social psychologists and experimental, what I sometimes call "rat," psychologists. But the experiments of social psychology have nothing to do with how rats are like people. They seek to discover, in controlled conditions of various kinds (rooms, with one-way mirrors, social-group pressure) how one person is affected by another, by group values, and by wider social values.

Some sociologists are now beginning to venture into areas that combine *art and sociology*, such as photography, or the writing of plays for sociological criticism.[25] Some sociologists who are heavily statistical in their own work disregard these new efforts or refuse to admit them as legitimate. Others, including some whose personal preferences are for quantitative research but who enjoy reading this style almost as a hobby, approve and encourage the new developments.

I could go on and on, but the variety of approaches and mixes of approaches should be apparent by now. There is also much variety in terms of how involved a particular sociologist gets. Some stay at the university, othrs do consulting, still others are right at the forefront of social action and political strategy making. Sociology, then, is as broad and complex a field when you look at what sociologists do as it is when you look at the subject matter. What makes it one field, none the less, is the ability and desire of its workers, however broad or narrow their approach, to comment in some way on our social existence in general, to see the whole in the part.

A Plan for the Book

We began by considering a rather basic question, Why study anything? Historically, sociology could not have come into being until people were ready and willing to look at the natural world and then the social world, as an object of curiosity. When they began to get the idea that more than one social world was possible, points of view were increasingly presented on what the desirable society should look like. The next step was that of the founders, such as Comte and Marx, who had the goal of a theory, a model of what actual societies really were like, how they were put together, and where they were heading and why. Defining the field became a problem from the start. Choosing a research approach became an issue as well.

In this book I cannot possibly cover all the ground that sociologists cover, or cover all points of view. (It should already be clear that not all sociologists have the same social point of view or agree on the role of sociology, its scope, or even what a sociological study *is*.) But let me say clearly where I stand, at the start; that will give you perspective for looking at the rest of what I have to say. First, I think, a strong sense of history is necessary in looking at any sociological topic, for only in time depth do we get an idea of the directions social actors are going in, the ways social processes are developing. So we will look at the history of each broad topic area. Second, I think that any sociologist must take a stand on the findings discovered. I will be critical of both sociology and the social arrangements discussed in may cases. You should not always expect to agree with me. What is needed is a raising of some issues. You'll have the rest of your life to explore them in greater detail.

A third point involves the strategy for introducing the main areas of sociology. A natural way to proceed is to start with the individual's self-image, then go out to the next circle and investigate relationships between the individual and others. The two are related, of course, but we need to begin with how people view themselves in their own life cycles. After looking at the sociology of relationships, we will look at the careers people develop—the world of work viewed from the biographical angle. Next, out into the local community—what is worth investigating about this broad social unit? Following this, the issue of acting politically—your response to the social world you live in. We will conclude by considering the skill I hope you will develop with time—thinking sociologically.

One last issue is that of your motive for reading and mine for writing. In each area I'll end the discussion with a "So what?" section —an attempt to answer the question of what can be gained personally from studying a particular area within sociology, I don't mean selfish individual gain. Quite the reverse. If this book works, you will be nagged, urged, aroused, or bothered into going further in your study of the field and then, with a real and practical grasp of the facts of the social world apart from yourself, acting to change some of the facts for the better. There's no immediate hurry, though, and there is a long way to go first.

The beginning step is toward a deeper and more sociological understanding of how you came to be yourself.

For Further Reading

Gilbert Highet. *The Immortal Profession: The Joys of Teaching and Learning.*
New York: McKay, 1976.
A fascinating account of learning as an adventure and the ups and downs
of teaching, written by one of the masters in that field.

Walter Ullmann. *Individual and Society in the Middle Ages.* Baltimore: Johns
Hopkins University Press, 1966.
Short, scholarly, and well written, this book will get the complex world
of the Middle Ages across to any interested reader.

Harlan Lane. *The Wild Boy of Aveyron.* Cambridge, Mass.: Harvard University Press, 1977.
What is human nature? Lane recounts the excitement and the heartbreak
of the case of the wild boy of Aveyron. The book is also good on the
rehabilitation of handicapped children.

Lewis A. Coser. *Masters of Sociological Thought.* 2nd ed. New York: Harcourt,
Brace, Jovanovich 1977.
Each of the greats—Comte, Marx, Georg Simmel, Durkheim, and others
—written up as people and as theorists and set into their own historical
period. Clearly written introduction to social theory.

Patricia M. Golden. *The Research Experience.* Boston: Peacock, 1977.
Interviews with researchers working in each sociological style. They discuss how they do their kind of work, the problems they have, what it feels
like to do it, and why it is important.

Stephan Thernstrom. *Poverty and Progress: Social Mobility in a Nineteenth
Century City,* Cambridge, Mass: Harvard University Press, 1964.
A historian uses a sociological style of research to study Newburyport,
about four miles downriver from my home. A correction, from a later point
in time, of a study of the city in the 1930s.

Chapter

ONE

Discovering Yourself

One of the easiest mistakes to make involves self-knowledge. "Of course I know who I am and how I got that way" most people will respond if asked. One of the first tasks of a sociological inspection involves a second look at statements like this. In this chapter we will reinspect the process of becoming social—the way in which each society takes the helpless infant and eventaully forms the grown adult. We will consider how school plays a critical role in this process, especially in the area of lifelong self-esteem. Also, a sense of one's whole self—a sense of identity—develops through the entire life cycle from childhood through adolescence, maturity, and old age, and we'll review this process. We will use women's experience in a particular period in our own American history to get a sense of the importance of the social context to what we think of ourselves. We will conclude with a review of the possible uses of sociology for self-exploration.

Becoming a Social Creature

There was a time before we were separated from anything, before we were ourselves. Some people, in the grip of mystical experience or meditation or even immersed in a warm bath have relived this experience—or think they have at least. It is the time in the womb, a time broken with at birth (and, some are saying, not helped by the cruel

22

and quite unnecessary spanks of the obstetrician on the rear end of the new baby under the bright lights of a modern operating suite). Almost from the moment of birth we begin to develop a *sense of physical self*. Touch the table. Now touch your teeth with your thumb. The first time you felt the table, period. But the second time your teeth felt your thumb. And vice versa—your thumb felt your teeth. This is an example of the difference between all that we experience as "inside," and what we experience as "outside." The body image, all that we experience as "inside," is a basic part of our self which develops slowly over time.[1] The growth of our nervous system gives us a physical sense of boundaries as it develops. But finding out where your body ends and the wall begins is a process of trial and error, as any baby can demonstrate.

Sociologists call the process by which the biological infant eventually becomes a social creature the process of *socialization*. In total it is the process by which the norms, rules, values, and behavior patterns of the parents and the society of those parents are built into the child, so that they seem normal as ways of acting to the individual, as guides to thought and action. Socialization is a lifelong process. We will review here some early steps along the way: the formation of emotional bonds to parent figures, the acquiring of language, the development of personality and a conscience, the role of the family in developing a sense of self, and the development of self-concepts in the social setting as a consequence of relationships with others.

Infants respond very early to a relationship. The emotional bond to the mothering person is, for all of us, our first social relationship. Before speech, long before, the bond is already very strong:

> Children express their attachment to their mothers in different ways. Some want lots of cuddling and holding, others like to stay close to their mothers and need a lot of attention but don't want to be held, others are happy wandering away from their mothers but are delighted by looks and "conversation". . . . We need to distinguish between the *expression of attachment* and the underlying *attachment bond*.[2]

This bond is the rope on which the child will be pulled up the ladder from instinctive creature to social human being.

Acquiring language, the next great step in becoming social involves the coming together of biological equipment and a necessary social milieu. It doesn't matter what race the child is or what culture. Whatever language that first mothering person speaks, constantly and lovingly, the child will gradually pick it up. Recent discoveries show that the grammar of a language is learned a lot earlier than we might think. First there are random sounds, then the sounds get closer to the sounds of the mother. There is no meaning yet. Then, come the first words. At the point when the first two-word sentences are put together, what we have is the first grammar.[3] Research is indicating, in other words, that thought patterns are learned far earlier than we had at first expected.

This process of socialization, of becoming social, of developing a self that can be seen to be a part of a collection of selves called a society, has been approached by different kinds of theorists. They speak in ways that highlight different aspects of what is a highly complicated process though it seems automatic. People can see that it is complex instead of automatic only when it goes off the track.

Some nonsociologists help us understand this process. For example, the great depth psychologist Sigmund Freud proposed three mental functions, which could work together but which could sometimes be in conflict; they were named "the id," "the ego," and "the superego," though that makes them seem like things when they are really kinds of mental activity that we could better call "id-ing," "ego-ing," and "superego-ing." "The id" was Freud's term for our basic biological urges—strong and never really going away. "The ego" was his name for the central activities of mental functioning such as thinking, choosing, acting, speaking, and defending yourself against information that you don't want to hear. "The superego", the third and most directly sociological mental function, was the conscience, the moral rules of society built into the personality and functioning to say yes to duty and no to forbidden pleasure. Or it would make pleasure-bound people feel guilty if they went ahead anyway.[4] The sociological view is related to this system that Freud proposed, but its center of attention is elsewhere—on society and not on the psyche of the individual. Sociology focuses on the sources of the rules—the origins of the yeses and noes. Becoming social involves learning the specific rules of a society and having them become part and parcel of your own mental equipment. Note the small child with the ability to take small things. Imagine the child enlarged to the size of a six-foot adult without having learned right from wrong. Observe the monster child killing a brother for a crust of bread. This is precisely the classic definition of the psychopath, the legally insane defendant in a murder trial. No social rules built in, no social creature.[5]

Emile Durkheim was much interested in the society-wide consequences of this process of socialization. He noted that the moral order, or what he called the "collective conscience" of a society, was its overall degree of agreement on rights and wrongs. This order was society, to him. If people start to disagree over the basics, the society becomes *anomic*-a state of *anomie* exists where the moral order has broken down, and chaos rules. Thus socialization isn't necessary just for new individuals; it is what preserves the society in its present form, what conveys it from generation to generation.

We develop the sense of right and wrong from those close to us. Of course each culture will have some minor variations on the theme, but almost all will prohibit violence against one's immediate tribe, all will bar sex with one's parents, (except in a few cases in royal families), and all will encourage whatever behavior will result in the efficient production of the goods and services by which the society earns its livelihood. And of course there will be varying degrees of obedience to all the rules. All this is not an all-or-none proposition. Some people's superegos, or built-in social rules, are much stricter and better put together than other peoples'. In a more sociological terms, the existence of crime is testimony to the incompleteness of any society's moral order. (It is also, of course, related to how poor and desperate people are.)

The family is of course the natural setting for socialization. The *type* of family, whether two-generation or three-generation, whether single-parent or two-parent (or group commune); the ages and income level of the parents; the presence or absence of older and younger children in the home—all these factors affect the basic growth of personality and the development of self-image. All are of great interest to sociologists and social psychologists specializing in early childhood socialization. In addition, family life is the primary producer of broad-scale values, the guideposts for living and ideas of the desirable that are too abstract for small children but are gradually learned over the course of childhood.

Now what is necessary is to see if we can bring these ideas of social de velopment together in a theory of how it all happens. One early attempt to do this was made by a social philosopher at the University of Chicago who was taken up by the sociologists there in the early years of American sociology. He is our next topic.

The Self in Evolution: George Herbert Mead

An important theory, or model, for looking at the development of the self was invented by an unlikely person. He was a pragmatic philosopher with no apparent interest in sociology, but he became involved with a number of sociologists who were quite interested in leaving no stone—including him—unturned in pursuit of a perspective that would help them understand socialization and any changes in self-concept. The need for a theory to build a bridge between sociology and psychology had been highlighted by the work of other social psychologists of the time, and the word had gotten around the new sociology department at Chicago that Mead's lectures were quite interesting.

According to Mead, the functions of personality grow out of communication from one person to another. The functions or processes of the self as it evolves he calls the "I," the "me," and the "generalized other." Mead suggests this: Think of the center of consciousness as an "I." When this "I" looks outward, it sees that some people in the environment are of particular personal importance. It is as if the beacon from a searchlight shined out in the dark and hit a mirror surface, which shined the light back, the others are like reflectors on road signs at night lit up by your headlights. All of these reflectors back, all of these meaningful others, have this characteristic: they help to define your self-image—what Mead called your "me." They are the ones to whom you turn and who intrude on your thinking even sometimes when you would rather they didn't, volunteering answers to such implied questions as "What do you think of this act of mine?" and "Who am I to you?" and "What do you like about me?" These answers as recorded in your head eventually build your self-image. But you actively build it too. You interpret what you think the others meant when they talked about you. That is the other side of Mead's dynamic approach.[6]

What made Mead's approach unusual, and useful for this first generation of social psychology researchers in need of a theory, was his insistence that all three self-functions—the "I," the "me," and the "generalized other"—were developed in the process of relationship to others, and were in a state of change and evolution over time as a consequence of further social interaction between people. For example, your "I" acts and says "I love you" or "Go jump in the lake" to another person in your life. Mead called the "I" the great unpredictable essence of the personality, the source of action, change and innovation, capable always of a new kind of act. Your "me"—your image of yourself—is altered inevitably by the response from the other to what your "I" has just done. The more someone means to us, the more vulnerable we are to his or her opinions, which can change our self-image in spite of our attempts to say they won't.

A young psychiatrist at the University of Chicago, Harry Stack Sullivan, sat in on some of Mead's lectures during his training. Sullivan also became famous, and his first book, *The Interpersonal Theory of Psychiatry*, started a whole new strategy for helping mentally ill patients, especially severely disturbed schizophrenics. Sullivan found a way to put Mead's basic observations to practical use, especially the idea of self-development. With schizophrenics—people severely ill mentally and out of communication with others—there was hardly a self there in the first place, so Sullivan used Mead's insights to help to build one for people who did not have one. He noted that they had not put their "I" together and had a messed-up or incomplete "me," part of which they were willing to admit existed and part of which they said was "not me." What was needed, Sullivan observed, was an interpersonal theory of psychiatry that dealt with self-building and self-disturbance.[7]

The strategy for helping came from the diagnosis that the self was underdeveloped and the insight from Mead. Become a "significant other" to a severely disturbed mental patient first—to whatever part of the patient's "I" can see you there. Help the patient put the "I" together by supporting its feeble attempts to think and act. Help such patients deal with awful images of themselves that were usually ground into them, in many cases by cruel and unloving ones close to them at home. This process of interaction, Sullivan noted, could help in the first place to tear down a distorted self. The reverse would take much longer, but would also have to be done in interaction, face to face, with great patience and much love and understanding. What goes for the ill goes equally well for the normal. This theory of self-development is a *social* psychology because it focuses on the social relations between you and others, the ones that help to build your self in the first place.

There is a caution here, and a moral. Freud, Mead, and Sullivan were not interested in developing an approach of blaming the others. In the end, a person is still his or her own responsibility. Understanding what others have done to your self-image—tear it down, or perhaps inflate it unreasonably—does not excuse you from the responsibility of acting yourself to better your situation, and those of others. But for those of us who are in deep personal trouble this social psychological way of thinking allows insights that are simply lost if all we do is react blindly to the people before us instead of asking *why*.

School and the Spiral of Self-Esteem

In colonial times, the vast majority of the people did not go to school from childhood to maturity, and indeed it was routine for many females not to receive any formal schooling. After the American revolution, however, and as part of the flowering of the great new American experiment, popular short-term public education spread. Literacy, simple ability to read and write, became nearly universal among adults by 1830 or so for both men and women, and from this point on, the school experience became central. Time passed. Then, later in this century, as the first great waves of immigration from Ireland and from the non-English-speaking world hit our shores, school took on all kinds of important tasks that it had not undertaken before. Lawrence Cremin, a historian of American education, notes that the shift to city living in the 1830 to 1880 era had led, by 1876, to the growth of many urban schools, providing an experience already more like that of today than that of the two centuries before.

More important, the expectations of what school could do for people and for the society grew and grew, in

> . . . the great nineteenth century shift in which the institutions of schooling and rehabilitation became the chief educational instruments of public policy and political development. That tendency became more pronounced during the twentieth century, as Americans placed broader and heavier responsibilities on public schools, public prisons, public reformatories, public child guidance clinics, and the like.[8]

What are the true social functions of school? As most of those who have studied schools will agree, information is only one part of what is conveyed. Socialization in general is of greater importance. Most American schools convey the middle-class values of striving for success, conformity, productivity, quiet hard work, and obedience to authority, here that of the teacher. Children who get the message at home are quite likely to feel comfortable at school and know "how to act," meaning how to act in a way that the teacher will approve.[9] In observing small children in elementary school classrooms not long ago (while professionally evaluating a program to place handicapped children in regular class), I was struck by the ease with which children of professionals and executives fit into the routine of first grade. The children of working class or welfare parents tend to be just as bright as the others but more boisterous and less reading oriented. These children often feel out of place in the classroom, and first-grade teachers, who typically are inexperienced and overburdened, often don't know how to help them. Occasionally the teachers get mad and these children are told in no uncertain terms that they aren't wanted.

What school does to children's self-esteem and feelings of worth, as well as their faith in the use of education for advancement, thus quickly becomes social-class-related. For the middle class child school is an opportunity to show off what was already learned at home, and to develop a sense of competence at work. Learning and experiments at home, with extra toys and encouragement from parents, lead to a confidence about ability, an attitude of "look what I can do." So achievement becomes a big thing in life, for child as for middle-class parent.[10]

The other side of this coin is the usual fate of the child in the ghetto school, or the docile working-class child in a high-pressure public school oriented to college and success. Jonathan Kozol notes what happened to the black children in a poverty-area school where he was a substitute teacher:

> You could not mistake the absolute assumption that this mess was not only their own fault but something to be ashamed of ... The place was ugly, noisy, rotten. Yet the children before me found it natural and automatic to accept as normal the school's structural inadequacies and to incorporate them, as it were, right into themselves.[11]

With the upper-class or middle-class child in the supportive school, an upward spiral of self-esteem develops. A sense of success leads early to inner self-confidence, the self-image of "I can do it," the willingness to try again because of the praise received. The reverse happens to children who are ignored or told they do not fit in, perhaps because of racism or other prejudice of the teacher. They have a downward spiral of self-esteem, in which early failure leads to lower self-esteem, unwillingness to try hard, and thus further failure. The failure is hard to take. If it is recorded, the students begin to stand out—to get *noticed* as failures. When noticed, such children often rebel or retreat into a robot-like kind of behavior. They can become sullen, prisoners of the classroom. Again, this may have little or nothing to do with basic ability. Yet quite early in the game—recent research suggests by grade three or so—the class system of the wider society is becoming visible in the classroom.

During the antipoverty program of the mid-1960s the U.S. Office of Educational Opportunity Head Start program tried to reverse this downward spiral of self-esteem in children. First, the program carefully chose as teachers only people who really liked poor children, and especially black and Puerto Rican poor children. Then modern educational techniques were tried that would not make these children feel out of place. These were also used on national educational television on the *Sesame Street* program. The idea was that learning can be fun—and that nice adults who like kids, including kids who bounce around and are active, can help them overcome fear and self-doubt.

Wonders were worked with those few children exposed to these programs.[12] But the long-term results of this approach are critically important in understanding how schools usually function as a preserver of the social status quo rather than increase chances for the poor and working class. First, though a kindergarten or a summer program might be changed into a Head Start-style class, the typical urban school had few funds to innovate with, and a fair number of schools had racist, tenured teachers. Other teachers, who did try, soon became bewildered and tired, and lost interest. One evaluation of the Head Start program of the Office of Economic Opportunity, made in the late sixties, found the progress of the children undone in a year or so, since the regular school milieu of the next grades had not changed. It was titled, "Head Start to Oblivion."

As important as the problems with the Head Start program itself were some findings on the use of the *Sesame Street* program. Originally it was funded by the Ford Foundation and OEO to create educational programming attractive to ghetto children. But some of their homes had no TV, or there were many children who would compete for the set and the smallest would lose out, or the crowded conditions made real concentration difficult. By contrast, large numbers of middle- and upper-class parents encouraged their children to watch *Sesame Street* religiously, and they did, and learned from it and had their questions answered at home. Ironically, the program became yet another thing that widened the educational distance between the bettter off children and the poor. This is not the whole story, of course. For example, black enrollment in college—children of the sixties becoming the college students of the seventies—has increased markedly. But many black college students come from middle-class homes, and the problems of poverty, as reflected in home conditions and the poverty-area school, remain. Meanwhile, out there in the suburbs the parents plan every step on the road by which Johnny or Mary will go to college.

Tracking: High and Low Roads in School

Tracking, or the grouping of children by ability remains quite common in most American public school systems. In their often quite theoretical and technical debates on this process most educators ignore its effects on the self-image of the children in the lower tracks. Tracking has started in earnest as early as the fifth or sixth grades in most American school systems. "Are you in the 'I' group or the "III' Group?" the ten and eleven-year-olds ask each other at the beginning of the school year. Furthermore, the teachers may act differently toward them depending on their group, having further effects on the self-esteem of these very sensitive preteen children. In my daughter's rather typical junior high school I have observed one teacher teaching a group of "III"s and then a group of "I"s the same subject two periods in succession. To the "III"s he was a barking, stern and, somewhat cold schoolmaster, almost scornful at times, at best a gruff, coaching camp counselor. They responded with fear. Some fidgeted, some gave back sullen conformity, occasionally there was a defiant acting-out behavior. In walked the "I"s a period later. To my surprise, the material was not that much different. But the teacher's behavior and tone changed. He was polite, helpful, quite calm. At one point he called a student "Miss." The children went at the work quietly, the teacher attended them at the side of their desks, something like a respectful wine steward at a fancy restaurant.

One case does not make an argument. But there is a classic experiment that proves this point clearly and unforgettably. Robert Rosenthal and Lenore Jacobson went into a school system, used a fake intelligence test, and told the teachers that one group of children (chosen at random from a hat) were going to make rapid improvements and be the stars of the classroom by the end of the year. At the end of the year the teacher in each classroom had spent extra time and given extra respect to these randomly chosen "stars." And they had indeed improved. The only catch was that the same could have been the case with any kid in the class. The expectations of the teachers and the attention and respect they gave these children demanded higher performance and the teachers supported them when they achieved it. In other words, the upward spiral can be created far more than it is. But this should ideally not be as the result of a trick. Why, for example, weren't the teachers looking at potential and demanding this kind of achievemment before the experiment?[13]

In more general terms, looking at the process sociologically, the class system of the wider society and the children's acceptance of their low, medium, or high place within this system are often perpetuated through the schools. They act as a "sifting device" that prepares the next generation silently and gradually for success or failure out in the world after school is over. Not that there aren't exceptions —it is possible for the brilliant student to work his or her way out of the poorest slum into one of the nation's elite colleges. But on balance, poverty-level students get the worst schools in many ways, and wind up with the least challenges to develop their ability.

Finally, some very important things are learned early in school about being a citizen, about being a political actor in later life. I don't refer to the artificial claims that "schooling promotes good citizenship" or some such that are often mouthed as slogans by elementary and junior high school administrators and even more by high school principals. Rather, I mean the students learn the politics of survival, in the sense of learning where the power is, of learning how to deal effectively with the sometimes stupid or uncaring in positions of authority and power over one's life.[14] Again, the poor, minority-group members, and, often, female students are at a disadvantage in middle-class schools and the whole *school* is likely to be in poor shape if all the children in it are poor.

In general, the experience can be a cruel and deadening one, with only a rare lively teacher or administrator to relieve the monotony. Films made of life in the ordinary ghetto or working class high school suggest a milieu that is quite prisonlike in its regimentation, a milieu that seems to be preparing many students for a later life in the regimented factory or office atmosphere.[15] One learns here that it is no good to be a loser, or ugly, or different. Even people who have been great successes in later life still remember their times in such schools and bear emotional scars they got there for the rest of their lives.

Identity: A Sociological Critique

Another way to understand the growth of your idea of yourself is to think of the way you arrived at your overall sense of who you are at present—your sense of personal identity. This complex process has been of great concern to sociologists and to psychiatrists and psychologists with a special interest in the social context of personal development. Sociologists concentrate on the situation and on the evolution of people's sense of themselves as the situation evolves. They deal with people's attempts to control that situation and the ways in which the situation controls and has an impact on them. Psychologists tend to keep personal dynamics central. The social situation is brought in but studied less carefully. A whole army of researchers have worked in this area through the years. I have picked two as examples—Erving Goffman as a sociologist studying the evolution of self in situations and Erik Erikson the famous psychoanalyst on the unfolding of personality in context. There are things to criticize about the work of both, but both have much to say in this area.

Erving Goffman writes:

> By *personal identity* I have in mind . . . positive marks or identity pegs, and the unique combination of life history items that comes to be attached to the individual with the help of these pegs for his identity. Personal identity, then, has to do with the assumption that the individual can be differentiated from all others and that around this means of differentia-

tion a single continuous record of social facts can be attached, entangled, like candy floss, becoming then the sticky substance to which still other biographical facts can be attached.[16]

This gets at the fact that your uniqueness is in part socially defined and has social tags. *Stigma,* the book in which Goffman spoke thus of personal identity, is basically concerned with the self-image of the malformed and handicapped and how their definitions of themselves conflict and contrast with the way others typically define them. Goffman has been much concerned with the way people try to present themselves to others and to manage and form the impressions others have of them. He has often stayed on the surface of social events and the person-to-person dealings. But he is a master of this terrain, of the fleeting and shallow and routine ways we go "on stage" to an audience of others and try to change or form their impression of us, of the secrets and hidden truths covered up by the wallpaper of social relations as usually understood. Goffman has done a series of studies on such topics as behavior in public places and relations between therapists and patients ("facework"), the handicapped and the non-handicapped, and surgeons and nurses in operating suites. In them he pointed out that in all these situations a *social* definition of the relationships involved exists and has major consequences for the way individuals present themselves and eventually think of themselves as well. Most tragic are those who through no fault of their own are thrust into a situation that is set up to destroy the self. Goffman writes thus of a mental patient suddenly hospitalized against his will and the "betrayal funnel" of those who brought him to the locked ward:

> For the person to whom the patient turns for help—for protection against such threats as involuntary committment—is not just the person to whom the mediators and hosital administrators logically turn for authorization. It is understandable, then, that some patients will come to sense, at least for a time, that the closeness of a relationship tells nothing of its trustworthiness.[17]

Now let's turn to a psychology-centered view of the issue of identity. Adolescence, the time of transition from childhood to young adult, is a key time for the formation of identity. One of the best-known analysts of identity from the psychoanalytic viewpoint has been Erik Erikson. Unlike many in his field, he has also been quite interested in the social context in which the child goes through stages of development, grows to adulthood, and indeed moves through the entire life cycle. By critiquing his ideas, we can see what a more sociological perspective can do to correct some of the biases in them.

As a psychoanalyst particularly interested in the relationship between inner self-development and outer place in the society (a social niche, a job, a career), Erikson has observed that the dangers of adolescence are similar to those of the trapeze artist. The adolescent must let go of one high swing (the parents) in midair, fly through the air, and grasp another swing (an adult role in life). In more formal terms Erikson has said that the young person needs to feel a unity of inner self and outer place that Erikson calls "ego identity." He puts it this way:

> The sense of ego identity, then, is the accrued confidence that the inner sameness and continuity prepared in the past are matched by the sameness and continuity of one's meaning for others, as evidenced in the tangible promise of a career. The danger of this stage is role confusion. . . . In most instances . . . it is the inability to settle on an occupational identity which disturbs individual young people.[18]

This statement, like many others Erikson has made over the course of his career as a famous psychoanalytic thinker, is important for what it does not say as well as what it does say. As critics of his work observe, there is something rather individual-centered about much that he has written about the process of self-development. First, notice that Erikson is saying that it is the *youth's* problem if there is no meaningful way to work after school is over. Note what that means for the black ghetto youth or sixteen-year-old male graduate of an Indian school in New Mexico who can't find a decent job. He has the problem. Well, in one sense he has, but only because our society has dumped it in his lap. He jumped in mid-air, but society didn't push a trapeze swing out at all! Or take the problem of more than a million young American women every year who upon graduation from high school find their occupational choice llimited to something like a secretarial job in a factory or office. They have a chance for a new sense of identity, but with what consequences for self-fulfillment?

Another problem with the self-development model of Erikson is the lack of emphasis it gives to the power of society. This shows in the way he discusses rebels and innovators. Erikson has written biographies of Martin Luther, the founder of modern Protestantism, and Mahatma Gandhi, the great Indian who led that nation toward independence from Britain.[19] In these studies Erikson shows how the broad-scale development of history (the political and social conditions in late medieval Europe and in India under British rule) intersects with the life cycle of these particular men—how they were born "at the right time." He looks at their personal history—their relations with their parents, with school friends, and so on—and then tries to psychoanalyze their motives for acting as they did. They did act, of course, and made history. Erikson is fascinated, as are many others, by the rather upset or strange personalities that many such world-shakers have had. (There is a long list of books which study Hitler in this way.) A sociologist has problems with this way of thinking. Why? Because the presence of unusual people, who are born in any age, is not as important as change in social conditions, which gives these unusual people a chance to make a difference. Individuals have a major role to play—men do make history—but "they do not make it under conditions of their own making."[20]

In another study Erikson visits an Indian reservation in the American Southwest in the 1950s. He meets a lot of depressed Indian teen-agers and hopelessly alcoholic young Indian men. Erikson notes that this is just what you might expect, since they are in "role diffusion" and the society doesn't value them or give them a job. In the present, twenty years later, the Indians are more politicized and don't let psychoanalysts on the reservation. One of the sources of this change was the black power movement, which was born in Africa. The African movement's views were reflected especially well in the writings of the Algerian revolutionary psychiatrist Frantz Fanon. Writing about the Algerian revolution, he stated that the best psychiatric therapy for the oppressed is to strike down their oppressors, violently if necessary.[21] The ideas of the beauty of being black and the value of black history and tradition spread through all of Africa through the black power movement. And, in this country they helped to motivate or spur on American black activists such as Rap Brown, Stokely Carmichael, and Martin Luther King. They worked to organize black people politically and get them to strike back strongly at an unjust society. Most basically, out of the struggle black people began to develop a new sense of self-respect. They refused social roles thrust upon them and identities prepared for them and created their own. The American Indians, following this example, have organized. As this is being written they are suing to get back one-third of the state of Maine, and they have successfully pushed through new federal laws to give them control of their own schools and health care on reservations. New bumper stickers read "Custer Died For Your Sins."

Another example of the problem with giving people too passive a role in your theories about them is an illustration Erikson used in describing children's play with blocks. He noted that little girls tended to build rooms or houses, whereas little boys tended to build towers and engineering constructions that had height and length. From this he took off and began talking about the need for little boys to play at being men and related this to their sexual development—their phallic sexuality and future penis activity. The rooms little girls built he called a symbol for their own "inner space," that is, their future wombs, and their future role as wives, homemakers, and mothers.[22] This all went over without much of a hitch in the fifties when it was written. Then, as the women's liberation movement grew, people began to notice the element of sexism in Erikson's thinking. For instance, it occurred to them that little boys and girls make what they make with blocks because they tend to be given "male" and "female" toys by their parents and grandparents.

Erikson's mistake was to conclude, as he did, that children's sexual anatomy demanded a certain social future. Thus he wrongly concluded that the little girls' "inner space" was determining the way they, as women, would "naturally" and "inevitably" think about themselves and their identity or occupation. Freud, in turn-of-the-century Vienna, said, "Anatomy is destiny." At the time this tended to be true, but not because of anything biological. Rather, this was because of the near total bar against women in male occupations in Austria then. But if one believes that *now,* along with Erikson, one is "going against nature" to recommend certain futures for women. This important question is: Who is defining that nature for us, and what are the consequences if we refuse to go along with the definition, or if we *do* go along?

To sum up, the primary difference between perspectives of sociol-

ogy and depth psychology on identity lies in the attention that sociology pays to the context, the setting, the relationships, the social
forces and processes that affect the individual and go on to form the
sense of self. Erikson's attempt to bridge the gap between the points
of view is needed and is valuable. His failing is to accept the existing
society as a constant, a given, a background, instead of the real part
of personality and self that it is—an element in the formation of
identity and a powerful one at that.

For our next illustration of the social meaning of identity, let's turn
back the clock to the American past. We'll look at changes in women's concept of themselves that flowed from other changes in American life between the Revolution and the middle of the 1800's—the
period of a second American revolution, the revolution in our nation's industry.

Women's Image: America from Colonial Times to 1850

A social context, including economic arrangements and the way people produce goods and services has many effects on individuals.

The way work is set up—the division of labor—has as direct an
effect on self-image as the action of other individuals. Thus if there
is a change in the broad-scale social and economic arrangements in
a society, the way people view themselves is going to change as well.
Recent findings in the history of women in America show that the
common understanding of women's role changed during the period
from the Revolution to the mid-1800's, which was certainly a time
of broad-scale change in the nation. And the changes in views about
women in that period can help us understand much that is happening
for women today.

We can contrast the role of a pioneer woman in the colonial era,
on the farm, with a later image of women pushed by the mass media
of the time and widely accepted by middle-class women at home.
Dortha Bushnell, the colonial woman, was the basis of her family's
home economy:

> She was providing and training her six children, clothing her whole family
> in linens and woolens, spun, every thread, and made up in the house, also
> to a great extent by herself. She had a farm-and-dairy charge to adminis
> ter, also the farm workmen to board, and for five or six months in a year

the workers, besides, of a home-spun cloth-dressing shop. All this routine she kept moving in exact order and time, steady and clear as the astronomic year . . .[23]

This woman was described thus by her son. When *he* married, about 1830, after becoming a minister, the world had changed. A new industrial era had begun, and in its factories were made the things that Dortha Bushnell had made at home for herself and her family. This minister son of a pioneer woman married Mary Thorpe. His new bride was

> a woman of charm and education [who] sustained him in his chosen course. Her role, as he at any rate liked to conceive it, was the nurturing one of affection, not the disciplinary one of authority . . . His wife was to be his follower, instructing him as to his mistakes only by the pain they forced her to register. Insofar as she was to exert control over him, it was, as he once explained to her in a letter, to be an "influence." She would be felt, but not heard.[24]

Can you imagine Dortha Bushnell's husband speaking to her this way? Not very likely, for she was part of the basic two-person domestic, self-sufficient colonial economy, not an ornament and decoration like her son's wife. What had happened?

The answer is complex, but two prominent elements in it can be teased out of the web of happenings and trends over the fifty years from the Revolutionary period to the 1830s. First, in the changeover of the economy to the new capitalist order of the New England industrial revolution, a new consumer role for middle-class women was created. Second, the rise in literacy, as a matter of state policy, led in turn to the rise of a new mass culture. Cheap "weepy" women's novels became popular, and an alliance between their women authors and ministers developed. This group pushed a new image for women. They should be passive, up on a pedestal, and demure, not aggressive, and should praise their men and keep in the background, quiet and respectful. This was defined as "femininity." Finally, there was the creation of a sense of women's differentness, which led at first to a sense of sisterhood in suffering, but led, eventually, to some women taking their enforced sexual ghetto feelings and making out of them a sense of "women in struggle together." They began, in some instances, to fight first for the freedom of enslaved groups—such as the blacks—and then for their own rights. We can investigate each of these themes briefly.

A fork in the road developed with the building of the first great mills to make cotton cloth on the Merrimac River, in New England about 1825. For here, at the birth of America's industrial revolution, the new factory owners created a new role for farm women, especially young ones—the role of mill girl. The girls worked all day and half of Saturday; in their mill dormitories at night they were watched over by housemothers.[25] The excess wealth of the men of the rising business class and the new professionals who were their allies was spent by their rather different wives, the new women at home. They became the targets for the first great generation of advertisers, the ones who made up *Godey's Lady's Book,* which was the first woman's periodical in the United States, and then the first Sears catalogue. These women were ushered into a new world of ease, of manufactured gadgets, of finery for the woman as decoration and helper—but not, of course, the woman as maker of her own things. Most importantly, the consumer behavior of these women—to *buy* instead of to make—itself became necessary to support the growing world of industry, for if there aren't enough buyers for the things made in factories, then business fails.

Married working class women often continued work in the mills, for salaries were low. But they in addition also tried, on limited funds, the new role and the occasional purchase of a luxury. Particularly useful was their role as a kind of battlefield medic and nurse, patching up their battered and tired worker husband, after his ordeal in the factory, the mines, or somewhere else in the difficult "world of men" outside the home. The wealthier women were also supposed to do this therapy and soothing—with less pressure on them of course in comparison to the women working full time in the factory.

Ann Douglas has studied the women's books of the time and calls the period from the 1780s to the 1830s the time of the "feminization of American culture." By this she means that culture itself—in the sense of the arts, sensitivity to the feelings of others, and good manners and politeness—was increasingly defined by Protestant ministers and lady writers as "female" and contrasted with the "male" world of politics, fighting, cigars, and business.[26] What bothers Douglas and other critical historians is the clear evidence that an educated minority of educated women did this to their sisters. The clergy, a powerless clergy in need of allies and quite unlike the powerful early Puritan hell-and-damnation preachers, found women an audience and a source of social support.

Women were actually submitted to a mass media blitz lasting two generations, one which constantly and publicly urged them to think of themselves as *ideally* passive, emotional, and dependent, and to try to live out this ideal. This image and ideal was the new standard by which they were to measure their human success. Since it kept men comfortable and sold clothes, thereby helping to keep the economy on its tracks, it served its purpose in establishing a new status quo, a new social world. Of course, this all was achieved at tremendous cost to the self-esteem of women, who were pushed into a social and psychological ghetto, devalued as human beings, and limited in their opportunity.

Yet there were some other, better consequences. If such a thing happens to a group of people, they may turn first to self-support and then, in some cases at least, to action to change their definition of themselves and their situation. Education, the same education that set women up for the sentimental novels painting their new role, and which gave them the ability to read advertisements, also gave a few of them a broader view of the world. Sisterhood—female solidarity —grew precisely out of the oppression that had come from the way others were now defining women. Women's finishing schools bred a new generation of thinkers, such as the critic and social reformer Margaret Fuller. By the late 1830s', new women activists were already campaigning for the abolition of slavery—we ought to know, they said, we have hardly any legal rights either. For example, the Grimke sisters of Charleston, South Carolina, pushed for total female liberation in the 1840's.[27]

Slowly, more and more women came to realize that they were an oppressed group. The ultimate consequences for their self-image— and their political future—can be found as early as the beginning of the Victorian era. Nancy Cott sums it up this way:

"We are a band of sisters—we must have a sympathy for each others' woes," wrote a woman operative in the Voice of Industry in 1847, alluding to *women* workers when she mentioned "that class to which it is my lot to belong . . ." Not until they saw themselves thus classed by sex would women join to protest their sexual fate.[28]

Thus the roots of the women's liberation movement of today date from this earlier period. The same sociological principle is in action today as then. A group begins by rejecting the broader social definition of itself and acts to form a new one. Identity is not static—it is a social process.

Discovering Yourself: Some Sociological Strategies

A sociological approach can give us a series of insights into who we are, how we became who we are, and, most important of all, who we might become. From the first moments of life our image of ouselves, as well as our degree of trust or mistrust of others, is influenced by social relationships. The very idea of social rules and the content of whatever conscience we possess are learned at home in our very early years. So too are negative ideas about ourselves—for instance, that we are no good, or undesirable. It is necessary for us to review and remember what we were told about ourselves and the nature of the rules and the values we learned at home. We may ultimately agree or disagree with them. But it is first necessary to confront them, and realize that we could have learned and experienced other things at home that we did not. A rapidly growing field of sociology and social psychology is concerned with this early life experience. It can help with your questions.

Everyone has gone to school. What kind of school it was and the precise experiences you had there year after year need to be reviewed from a sociological perspective. Did you, for example, grow up in a privileged situation, or in the reverse? What were you taught about achievement, about your abilities? By now the experiences of elementary school, junior high school, and high school may have somewhat faded into the past, but something remains. More important, awareness of the brutal and unfair treatment many others have received while going through school should help you understand that dropping out or lack of interest in studies or not thinking clearly in class is not a simple problem. Study in this area of sociology should help you understand the role school plays in determining our life chances, often loading the dice. This study should also remove some pride you may take in your "natural intellectual superiority" to some of the classmates you left behind.

Every year that I teach introductory sociology I ask the class to indicate by a show of hands whether they were told, somewhere along the way, that they were not "college material." A third to a half of the hands in the room usually go up. And then I ask those who *took* the advice to raise *theirs*—and a flood of ghost non-students seems to appear in the minds of the class. Their friends who listened to the advice, who believed too easily. People can resist the definitions of themselves made by others when these definitions are unfair. Such definitions can hurt but they can be fought. Sociology studies the identity-forming process, especially how the existing society attempts to mold us and our ideas of ourselves to fit the slots that it has set up. The nation is full of stereotyped ideas on how the school system is supposed to work and who should be where in it. A ton of sociological studies awaits the reader who wishes to understand the way the system actually works and the consequences for students.

Racism and sexism are attacks upon ourselves, whether we are the attacker, the attacked, or a watcher on the sidelines. They can be fought in the long run by changing the social contexts in which they occur. A sociological approach to selves formed in specific social contexts will aid us in developing the knowledge of ways to change them. The example of what some black people and Indians have done is clear here, as are some past and present attempts by women to change their situations. We can come to see, from a sociological perspective, how economic interests, the mass media, and those put in the same social basket work as definers of selves. Most important of all, we can learn from a careful study of the past and present how we must change our opinions about ourselves and others as a first step in changing our world.

For Further Reading

Judy Dunn. *Distress and Comfort.* Cambridge, Mass.: Harvard University Press, 1977.
> Ups and downs in the formation of the first social bond, the one between mother and child. One of an outstanding series, *The Developing Child.*

Roger Brown. *A First Language:* The Early Stages. Cambridge, Mass.: Harvard University Press, 1973.
> The latest view of language development in children, from direct observations of children over several years.

Charles Brenner. *An Introduction to Psychoanalysis.* Garden City, N.Y.: Doubleday, 1974.

A clearly written introduction to the ideas developed by Freud and refined over the last fifty years. Inner conflict, social influence, and the development of personality are considered in depth.

George Herbert Mead. *Mind, Self, and Society.* Chicago: University of Chicago Press, 1964.

Not an easy work but very important. Mead was the founder of interaction-based social psychology, and his ideas started a school of research.

Lawrence A. Cremin. *Traditions of American Education.* New York: Basic Books, 1977.

The story of America's educational institutions—how they moved from the periphery to the center of our socialization experience, how they changed with the times.

Jonathan Kozol. *Death at an Early Age: The Destruction of the Hearts and Minds of Negro Children in the Boston Public Schools.* Boston: Houghton Mifflin, 1967.

You are in the classroom and school halls with Kozol, and here the pain of these children becomes real. (Ten years after publication, things here and in other like places haven't changed much.)

Robert Rosenthal and Lenore Jacobson. *Pygmalion in the Classroom: Teacher Expectation and Pupil's Intellectual Development.* New York: Holt, Rinehart and Winston, 1968.

This work describes a classic experiment on teachers' expectations about children and the ways in which this affects children's self-image, teachers' behavior, and the fate of the children in terms of achievement in school.

Erik Erikson. *Childhood and Society.* 2nd rev. ed. New York: Norton, 1963.

A modern classic on the fitting in, or lack of it, of individuals in a society's life cycle. In spite of some biases, very worthwhile as a study of the development of personality in society.

Ann Douglas. *The Feminization of American Culture.* New York: Knopf, 1977.

Nancy F. Cott. *The Bonds of Womanhood: "Woman's Sphere" in New England, 1780–1835.* New Haven, Conn.: Yale University Press, 1977.

Two detailed and well-told stories on the self-image of women in the transition from colonial to early industrial America. Douglas is outstanding on the role of the communications media and the clergy. Cott is equally so on the meanings of sisterhood to the women themselves, including its outcomes in militant action.

Chapter

TWO

Understanding Relationships

There are people who have always lived in a supportive family, with stable and ever-loving parents, whose youth, adolescence, and maturity have been filled with a series of always meaningful, permanent, and rewarding relationships. These relationships have not been subject to social stress, to disillusion, pain and termination. And then there are the rest of us—most of us, I suspect. What can sociology tell us that thousands of years of puzzling over the mystery of human relationships have not been able to tell us? Not all we need to know, it should be said in the beginning. For each relationship has a unique history and course. No two are alike, nor is the same relationship really the same from day to day.

Sociology is the study of social regularities, of things shared from person to person and do not all human relationships, unique as they are, nevertheless share certain features? They do, and a sociological approach will help in understanding them—the relationships we are presently in, those we have had in the past, and those we might form in the future. In this chapter, then, we will explore some sociological dimensions of relationships. First, we will explore their geometry - the structure and shape of social bonding. Next, the concept of "roles" will be explored as a way of seeing how people set up their relationships with one another. After this we'll consider the power dimension of relationships and how the power can be misused. Then I'll take up how our relations with others, especially within the family, are not the same as they were in the past or are likely to be in the future. I'll conclude the chapter with a review of the things you might gain from a long-term study of sociology of human ties.

Hermits, Triangles, and Strangers: On Social Geometry

Everyone has seen a tall building in its early stages of construction. The steel girders make a neat geometric sketch of the finished building; they are a skeleton of the final product. It is possible to look at social relationships in a similar way, as a set of structures, a skeleton of forms, a network of bonds. A *group*—an arrangement of people sharing something, existing over time—has a *structure* and a *form*. It makes a difference, for example, whether we are talking about one person or two or three, or more. Consider the hermit. Georg Simmel, a sociologist who specialized in the study of social arrangements, observed that a hermit, a social isolate, *does* have mental relationships with others, even when "alone":

> Isolation, insofar as it is important to the individual, refers by no means only to the absence of society. On the contrary, the idea involves the somehow imagined, but then rejected, existence of society. Isolation attains its unequivocal, positive significance only as *society's effect at a distance*—whether lingering of past relations, as anticipation of future contacts, as nostalgia, or as an intentional turning away from society.[1]

In other words, a hermit is making a social statement, which implies relationship to others out there toward whom the "hermiting" is directed. The last man on earth is not a hermit. He is simply alone.

The *dyad*, or two-person group, is the elementary building block of relationships. Almost all children begin with one person as an "other." In modern arrangements, more fathers are sharing this experience. Long-standing close two-person relationships can have great payoffs for the two people involved, but the people also run great risks. The greatest risk is the vulnerability of each. Either person can end a dyad, and that's that. It always takes two to tango—the thought of the possible end of the relationship lends a particularly poignant quality to the life of it. Given the divorce rate at present, even ordinary marriage has a lot of this feel. Other risks of the dyad are trivialness and boredom, which can come from sharing so much of life, and putting so many of our emotional eggs in the other's basket, that one false move from the basket and all the eggs go crashing to the floor. This is why marriage counselors, for instance, usually encourage young married couples to form or to keep up relationships outside the one they have with one another. *Friends,* rather than lovers, are usually recommended of course!

To change a dyad to a *triad* or triangle by adding a third person adds a distinctly new element to relationships and sets up a whole new range of dynamics. As Simmel put it, the three-person group is different from any two-person group because

> No matter how close a triad may be, there is always the occasion on which two of the three members regard the third as an intruder. The reason may be the mere fact that he shares in certain moods which can unfold in all their intensity and tenderness only when two can meet without distraction: the sensitive union of two is always irritated by the spectator.[2]

Or, less elegantly, two's company, three's a crowd. In addition to the difference in intimacy, there are the politics of triangles. Any triangle can dissolve at any moment into a temporary or a permanent two-against-one situation. Sensing this, people have trouble even when things ought to be going well.

Several types of strategies are used by people who want to manipulate the triangle setup. For example, a person may set up a triangle to get the other two people to compete for his or her attention. An event in the recent past in international politics was the attempt— successful as it turned out—by Henry Kissinger and President Nixon to set up relations with China. The idea was to get both the Soviet Union and China pushing to be our friends in order to make them even more competitive and suspicious of each other than they already were. There is another kind of third position—the mediator. Here the third tries to get the other two to settle their differences. But this is a risky kind of triad, whether it is the U.S.-Arab-Israeli relationship or the situation of John, Jim, and Mary.

After three people we are dealing with groups without such clear geometrical properties. But in all of these, certain arrangements are of interest. An example is the *secret society.* The U.S. Central Intelligence Agency, the Klu Klux Klan, and the Mafia are all secret societies to some extent. Of course at the same time they are different in many ways, but all share the formal property of refusing to release information on their secret life.[3]

Finally, there is the position of the *stranger*. Simmel called the stranger "that member of a social group who is outside it, in active confrontation." Who has not been in this position at some time or other? Being a stranger is different for each of us, but we all share something as a consequence of having experienced it. In general, the number and social geometry of group arrangements can tell us some basic things about the experience we are likely to have in them.[4]

The Social Bond: Depth, Dynamics, Quality

Our dog, a collie named Laddie, sometimes bothers the cats. He is usually scolded for this, because the cats are annoyed even if Laddie is only trying to be friendly. A sharp word sends him scuffling around the room in a wide circle. Then he will come over to you, sit down, and hold up his paw. He holds it up not to shake your hand, but to *hold* your hand. He lowers his long nose and looks up. The look in his eye is unmistakable. It says, "Do you still love me?" Relationships do not have to be between two people, and when they go across the lines of the animal kingdom, they usually are on a more basic level. The nonverbal, visual, and emotional ties that we have to our pets can stand as an example of the kinds of primitive communication that exist between people in any relationship. Body language—the way we sit, stand, and gesture—and tone of voice are two elements of this kind of interpersonal communication. But among human beings other extremely complicated elements arise. These involve our ability to remember past experience in each relationship, our ability to use language, and the mysterious process called empathy, a key to the depth of any relationship.[5]

To begin with, time is a dimension of any relationship, and we are storers of experience. If that experience has been good, rewarding, and enlivening, then it will tend to lead to further exchanges; if it has been a bad experience, it will stand as a barrier against a deep relationship in the future. One of the characteristics of some cheap and I think trivial group counseling that is advertised today is that it promises the instant wiping away of all past troubles, clean slates, and the total and instant renewal of relationships with the erasing of memories. If we were tape recorders with an erase button, maybe so, but we aren't. Beyond this, some people are coming to believe that they have a right to their experience, even the worst side of it, and don't want anyone to take it away. The past of relationships must influence the present, so it is in the present that we build our future ties.

The use of language—in words, gestures, and bodily movements —is a second index of the depth of a relationship. Some people can be married to their spouses for twenty years and still speak the language of strangers. They can talk to each other like formal debaters or bargainers at a conference table. Others speak in a code with lightening-fast references. Their talk is full of phrases that exclude the world and definitely seem a little impolite if used too much in front of others. Still others persist in the public display of emotions —kissing in a stagey way on the corner—which often convinces onlookers that the couple may not be too sure of their relationship. And, there are the dimensions of "language" exchanged in relationships which are not verbal, but add the color, even the real meaning, to any exchange. For example, try to say "really" to someone else in as many different ways as you can. Body language, is often a dimension of the relationship that the partners don't recognize. But it is there just the same, like a ground bass running in the background of a jazz composition.

Empathy is a third complex, almost mystical dimension of a true relationship. Empathy is the ability to put ourselves into the shoes of the other person or persons. It is not a talent shared by all to the same degree and in times of inner turmoil even people who have the gift in abundance lose some of it. Yet two egomaniacs conversing does not constitute a relationship. What *does* constitute one will depend, of course, on the extent of our needs and experiences and those of the other person or persons. The criterion of empathy is a tough one, but it is, I think, really necessary if what we mean is a relationship and not a formal acquaintanceship or two ships passing in the night.

The dynamics of relationships in groups have become a special area of study in sociology. Groups of people are brought together to work on a task. Then the sociologists observe the ways the people relate to one another to see what can be learned about the regularities. A classic example of this kind of work is that of Freed Bales and his coworkers.[6] Over the past twenty years they have been observing group activity behind a one-way mirror and recording the nature of the activity with a specially devised scoring scheme. A brief review of this scoring scheme can highlight some complexities that are involved when the number of relationships is multiplied in a group setting and the relationships develop over time. Each sentence spoken between two group members is recorded by number. For example, 3–4 might mean"Susan talks to Jim." Then a letter or other code sums up the quality of the little piece of interaction. Four main groups of action are coded: "positive reactions" (giving help, sharing, joking and agreeing); "questions" (asking for information asking for evaluation and analysis, asking for signs and direction); "attempted answers" (giving direction, giving opinion and evaluation, giving information); and "negative reactions" (disagreeing, withdrawing from activity, anger and aggressiveness to others.) What Bales and his associates found was that every group soon develops roles for the members. One may be the "task leader," another the "emotional leader," somewhat like the social director at a summer camp.

In general, the study of group interaction is simply one kind of research on the nature of relationships, from the social point of view. But the concern this approach has with *roles* within groups has another important message. It is to remind us that all relationships that last for any period of time develop a set of rules on how the people will behave with respect to one another and within the society in which they live. These roles, and the way people agree or disagree with one another in defining them, are our next concern.

Roles: On Stage and Off

Sociologists often speak of "roles"—a term that shares something with the language of the stage. If we inspect the dramatic idea of a role first, we can get a more practical idea of the sociological use of the term. In working on a play, one early step is to read the play through and try to understand how the words ought to sound when spoken by the play's characters on the stage. This process of "creating the role," or giving life on stage to the words of the playwright, was discussed by the great director Constantin Stanislavsky:

> The verbal text of a play, especially one by a genius, is the manifestation of the clarity, the subtlety, the concrete power to express invisible thoughts and feelings of the author himself. Inside each and every word

there is an emotion, a thought, that produced the word and justifies its being there. Empty words are like nutshells without meat, concepts without content; they are not used, indeed they are harmful. They weigh down a role, blur its design; they must be thrown out like so much trash. Until theater is able to fill out each word of the text with live emotions, the text of his role will remain dead.[7]

Put yourself in the position of an actor trying out for a play. You are on stage in an empty theater, holding the script in one hand. Stanislavsky is out there slouched in the tenth row. Each line you speak—and your overall interpretation of the part in the play—is or is not going to meet with the expectations and standards of the great Stanislavsky. He has a clear idea of how the role should be brought to life, how the part should be played. You have an idea also, but do your ideas match? And what would the playwright say about your interpretation, or Stanislavsky's?

As Shakespeare said, "All the world's a stage, and all the men and women merely players."[8] Social roles, the parts we play in the everyday drama of life, are interpreted by each of us as we go along. Some parts we know well; others are harder to understand. Who is the playwright? Society—that's who. And who is Stanislavsky? We are, to one another. I have an idea of how "father" is to be played. If it agrees with the role as written for my corner of the world by the wider society around me, and if my children and my wife expect the role to be played pretty much the way I'm playing it, then the show goes on without too much of a hitch. If we disagree about the role, trouble starts. But now we need to look at some differences between the stage and real life, for in the differences lie much of what we understand by the term "role" sociologically.

A sociological definition of *role* would be about as follows: the pattern of expectations, attitudes, and behavior in a shaped form, which that person or group has of another, concerning a particular social situation in which they both are present. Also, social roles have boundaries, they are related to social situations, and we can conform to our roles or "go out of role." There are some differences between stage roles and social roles. To begin with, most of our social roles are not written down on paper (except by sociologists!) In practice, we have a general idea on how to act in each social situation. If it is a work role we may have been given some training on how to act in it. In an earlier era, etiquette books provided a set of rules on just how to act in order to play the part of "lady" or "gentleman." Second, modern social roles tend to be changing at a faster rate than at many times in the past. Our era is somewhat similar to a drama where, after getting your lines down and your part to please both yourself and Stanislavsky, out dashes the play's *author* from the wings, crying "I've rewritten your part for this act." Third, although we play some roles just for the fun of it, at a party for example, many of the roles are very real and serious indeed. We may actually have "scripts"— laws with police and courts backing them up, telling us firmly how we may and may not act as "father," "wife", or "doctor." In almost all cases, though, it is us as ourselves on the line, rather than ourselves as actors. This is not to say that we don't have to fake it at times. But our emotions, self-esteem, and very position in society are often tied up in the roles we "play." Sometimes we try to distance ourselves from our own roles—"This isn't *really* me, just my job as a nightclub bouncer." But nightclub bouncers get depressed about themselves sometimes- the distancing doesn't always work.

Another part of the analogy from the stage lies in the double audience which every role has—yourself and the other observer or observers. If you play actor, they play audience. For your "father" there should normally be a "child," for some in the "doctor" role, there should be someone in a "patient" role. Roles, in other words, are ways of joining people together, with expectations of one another that may not be identical but that make sense together. This has immediate implications if we want to change a role. Stanislavsky out there—your child, your boss—is sure to scream. In totalitarian societies very few people can rewrite their roles. I'll never forget the time a group of younger sociologists, including myself, once held a sort of counterconvention to criticize the conservatism of the sessions at the Seventh World Congress of Sociology, in Varna, Bulgaria, in 1970. We tacked up signs in English, French, German, and Russian saying there was going to be a special session on "The Sociology of Sociologists," in the cocktail lounge on the fifteenth floor of the main convention hotel. One older Russian sociologist was more than a little upset at this innovative and disrespectful role for younger academics. Perhaps he also wondered what might happen to him if he attended —there were some mysterious "observers" around. He wagged his finger at us as we taped the signs up all over the lobby and in all the elevators. "Nye programmi! Nye programmi!" ("It's not on the *program!*") he commented angrily.[9]

This gets us to the key issue—who writes the roles? If you decide to change a role, being tied into other peoples' expectations is bound to cause a stir. For others in turn set their roles up in response to yours. Broad-scale historical forces at work may help to rewrite roles. They may even eliminate some, such as the role of the lamplighter. Or roles may be reinterpreted by a group of people who self-consciously feel that an author gave them an unfulfilling part to play. No matter what this author says or what numberless Stanislavskys on the scene say, the role will be redefined, redone, replayed, and the devil with the consequences. Women, blacks, gay people, Indians - any group of people redefining their role at present do so by refusing to accept the battered old script used in so many past plays. They thumb their noses at the various audiences of husbands, wives, lovers, bosses, and people who don't belong to minority groups. One thing giving our present historical period its importance is precisely the fact that so much of this is happening. So many people are taking the right to create their own roles into their own hands and combining with friends who agree to support their new role, that to do this is getting to characterize our age.

Situations help to define roles. Which theater the play is produced in does make a difference. For example, it is a lot easier to understand colonial life and colonial roles when you live through the long northern New England winters as my family and I do. In the evening we sit on two sofas in front of an old eight-foot colonial fireplace in the big "keeping room" (combination kitchen and family room) at the rear of the old house we live in. The two front rooms are shut off to keep the heat of the fire in the room we're in. Gathered around a low coffee table in from of the fire, the children do homework or make things or doodle. (I put some spotlights in the ceiling to help light this table and the sofas- it *is* the twentieth century.) I read or write. My wife may do likewise. The throwing together of people in this room creates a true social situation that does not necessarily demand much talking back and forth. The dog and the cats—Kim and Helen—lie down where I suppose such animals have always lain, in front of the fire. And yet the outside world is not cruel to us as it was to the people who lived here two hundred years ago, with the ravages of disease and the uncertainty of the crops they faced. So the situation can be only partly dictated by the scenery and setting.

There are times when the roles we play are actually *played*—that is, we are acting and know it. For example, Erving Goffman and others have studied "the presentation of self," and have noted the different ways in which we try at times to create an image, to make an impression, one that is not the same as the one we truly have of ourselves.[10] The dating bars around any college campus are a perfect stage for this kind of behavior. Another example is the difference between action "backstage," action "onstage," and the audience. In a restaurant the kitchen area into which the waitresses disappear is backstage, the table area is onstage, and the customers are the audience. Most participant observers of work in restaurants have noticed the steak being dropped on the floor in the kitchen and being dusted off. Then the server dashes onstage and delivers the steak to the diners with a flourish. In addition some situations are so strong that they may force you to change your idea of yourself, and the role you are playing begins to become a part of yourself even against your will. The Army has done this to some people. So have educational institutions. One student, Scott Turow, described the first year of Harvard Law School, in this way:

> For me, dealings with the faculty were complicated by the fact that only the year before I had been a teacher myself, up there in front of the classroom listened to, obeyed. Now I was in the seats, unheeded—in an assigned seat, in fact—with many details of my life controlled by other people. I began to sense that I'd been turned into a child again, an adolescent. With its murky corridors tiled in linoleum and lined with the lockers used by students who live off-campus, the law school has much of the look and smell of a high school, and there were an increasing number of moments when I really felt like a teenager, angry and adolescently rebellious. That was not a unique reaction.[11]

Turow goes on to note that a student rebellion occurred, especially because of treatment of students by one particular professor. The rebellion brought some changes to the law school but was not universally supported. Many were willing to put up with the role and insults from the professor, rather than attack the institution of Harvard Law School. Turow says that most students did not want to jeopardize the high payoff at the end of the educational road by developing a reputation as a troublemaker.

Make no mistake about it—this kind of situation, though a little extreme, is not unique. To change any set of roles is hard work. It take persistence, it often means opposing powerful and entrenched interests, and it doesn't always succeed. But one insight is important —there is no strong social playwright out there the way there used to be, at least not in *this* era, unless you are in a group presently boxed in by social prejudice and a strong overlay of tradition. If changing the roles will not hurt others—or even if they will but will free an oppressed group from an unbearable situation—then people can, and I personally think should, go ahead.

You have a responsibility if someone else is trying to change their role with respect to *you,* as well. No matter how strange or unsettling the action, the bystanders should at least try to put themselves in the shoes of those trying to change their roles. The homosexual or gay rights movement is an example. This is a group of people just asserting their right to their own way of making love and wanting not to be deprived of job opportunity or harassed by the police because of it. Yet look at the turmoil this attempt at role redefinition has caused. To reiterate, people can change roles, but the change in their roles often demands a change in our expectations of them as well, and *we* may not be ready. If sociology has any message concerning roles in this area, it is one about human rights—including the right, within some limits, to define your role yourself. Sociology also warns you that others may *never* be ready for you to do this, including those near and dear to you. Finally, sociology warns that the opposition may be more extreme and frightening than you expect.

Obedience to Authority: A Warning

There are reasons why we obey people. The issue of *authority* is basic here, one which Max Weber took up in detail.[12] He noted that there were different *types* of authority. If the police officer has his blue suit, badge, and cruiser, it is both his gun and the laws behind his gun that we obey. He is the bearer of *rational-legal authority*—the authority of the law, the courts, and so on. When the thousands followed Mohammed and Jesus, they did so at first on the basis of personal magnetism—*charisma. Charismatic authority*—in political leaders, in cult religious figures, in revolutionaries, in Popes—is always a key aspect of effectiveness and power. Some societies base the authority of their leaders on *tradition*—"Obey the king because your fathers and grandfathers did." The authority of established religions owes much to tradition. For example, Jesus was a charismatic leader, but the appeal of a Pope to the Catholic world lies at least in part in his being the head of a church that has stood for more than a thousand years. On the other hand, if the Pope is John XXIII or John Paul II, charisma is at least in part what makes for their authority and influence, far beyond the bounds of the members of the church itself.

A mixture of rational-legal authority, traditional authority, and charismatic authority tends to enter into any relationship of superior to inferior, or boss to worker, or parent to child. The question is, What is the mix? How are children socialized to react to authority situations, to authority relationships? To what extent are we really conscious of them? To what degree do we accept the legitimacy of this or that authority situation, without questioning or challenging it? What does it matter to us, anyway, in daily life? A lot, I think. Let's consider an example of this problem to show just how basic and important it really is.

Power and authority do not enter into all relationships to the same degree, of course. But our earliest ones, to parents, were definitely of the high power and high authority type, especially early in childhood. In those early years parents required our obedience in order to protect us from dangers we could hardly understand. Similar relationships continue for many people in our rather authoritarian schools, with less good reason. But this preparation may be the way a society teaches us to be comfortable in obeying the boss at work, even when the order being given is a stupid one. It may be that not enough of us are taught to question authority (that's *my* opinion, anyway) especially when it is ordering us to do things that our conscience warns us against. The authority giving orders to the less powerful often says, "I'll take the responsibility." This does dangerous things to many people's sense of right and wrong. It acts as an anaesthetic. Many Nazis claimed that they were only obeying orders in the systematic slaughter of Jews and others at the concentration camps in World War II. This problem surrounding obedience to authority has worried many social scientists. How many immoral and inhuman orders will people obey before they begin to rebel?

One researcher who did something about the problem was Stanley Milgram. In a series of experiments carried out at Yale University and other places he tested just this obedience situation with a sample of ordinary people—not college students. The people answered an ad in New Haven, Connecticut paper for a "teaching experiment." Milgram set up a "shock board" with a set of "electronic" switches, which were said to deliver electric shocks going from 150 to 400 volts. In the next room, visible through a window, the "student" (a grown man, an actor and an accomplice of Milgram's) was seated in a chair. The experiment "leader" who greeted the volunteers who had responded to the ad was *another* accomplice of Milgram's. He explained to the volunteer "teacher" that he was to read pairs of words to the student in the next room. He was to push the switches on the shock board if the student got the answers wrong. (Actually, there were no right answers—the test questions were phoney and any answer given by the student was going to be wrong, necessitating a shock.) The off-the-street volunteer was to shock the student for each wrong answer, and increase the voltage for each additional "wrong" answer. The "teacher" volunteer never knew that the shocks were phoney, and that the one shocked was faking his pain and agony at the "electricity." The whole thing was set up to see how far people would go before breaking off the experiment, in their role as shocker of innocent, suffering people.[13]

Sometimes the "teacher" began to get uneasy about the experiment, especially when the "shock victim" began to complain. The experimenter in the gray lab coat then said. "You *must* go on." He simply wouldn't take any excuse for quitting unless the "teacher" absolutely refused to continue. *Sixty-five percent of all those placed in the "teacher" role went all the way to the end of the shock board, even over the screams and protests of the "victim" in the next room.* Milgram observes:

> What is the limit of such obedience? At many points we attempted to establish a boundary. Cries from the victim were inserted; they were not good enough. The victim pleaded to be let free, and his answers no longer registered on the signal box; subjects continued to shock him. At the outset we had not conceived that such drastic procedures would be needed to generate disobedience, and each step was added only as the ineffectiveness of the earlier techniques became clear.[14]

Some variations on the experiment were developed. Was it the prestige of the Yale psychological laboratory that led the "teacher" to such extreme and ugly behavior? The experiment was moved to a plain office in Bridgeport, Connecticut, and no official tie to a university was indicated. Forty-nine percent of the subjects still went to the end of the shock board. Were men more obedient than women? The original group was all men. A group of all women was tried. Sixty-five percent, the same percentage as before, went to the end. But other variations did lead to significantly different results. The authority who is visible to the "teacher" is the man in the gray coat, who is introduced to the "teacher" at the start. If another person off the street is handed the gray coat and the "teacher" knows that this person is just another person like himself, then only 20 per cent of the "teachers" will go on shocking to the end of the board. If *two* gray-coat authorities disagree about whether the "teacher" should go on shocking the "student," and have an argument in front of the "teacher," no teacher goes on shocking.

Most illuminating of all is the contrast between the following two variations. In the first, a second "teacher" stands by the side of the shocker-teacher. When graycoat says go on, the second "teacher" then says, "No, no, don't do it!" and encourages resistance. In this setup only 10 percent of the shocker-teachers go to the end of the board. The second variation is ominous for all of us in what it may show about more ordinary social situations. The most successful arrangement was this: A "teacher" who is not in on the secret is put in the experiment as the one who reads the words out to the victim and then tells a second "teacher" to shock the victim. This second "teacher," who is in on the experiment, then pulls the switch. In this arrangement, the "teachers" off the street were "links in the chain of command." They were told to do the experiment by gray-coat then told someone else to pull the switch. Ninety-two percent of them kept on giving the order to shock to the end of the board. After being told about the true nature of the experiment, many of the people in this role said something like "Well, I just gave the orders which the man in a gray coat gave to me. *I* didn't pull any of the switches. . . ."[15]

Milgram had two somewhat related kinds of explanation for what he found. He said that evolution may have built a "turn-off-the-guilt" switch into each of us when we get into a chain-of-command situation. I don't buy this one at all, though you might disagree. If its automatic, then how do we explain the people who say *no*? The other explanation, which I *do* support, lies in the area of the legitimacy of authority. If an order is given by what we conceive to be a legitimate authority—or we do not want to cause trouble for ourselves and the ordergivers by saying no, which would be "impolite" and also make us stand out, we may go to amazing extremes. It is a *relationship* that is getting us into trouble, a relationship with an authority that we do not want to break. As Milgram puts it:

> The processes of obedience to authority . . . remain invariant so long as the basic condition for its occurrence exists: namely, that one is defined into a relationship with a person who one feels has, by virtue of his status, the right to prescribe behavior.[16]

That power relationship, based on one individual giving the legitimacy to the orders of a second, can blind the first individual to what he or she is doing. What is being done (the shocks, ignoring the cries of the victim) all proceeds from that original willingness to grant the authority his authority.

Another example of the power/obedience/authority issue comes from Vietnam. Roger Mudd of CBS is interviewing one of the soldiers who obeyed a front-line officer, Lieutenant Calley, who in turn claimed he had *his* orders from a higher rank officer:

> *Lieutenant Calley told me, he said, "Soldier, we got another job to do." And so he walked over to the people, and he started pushing them off and started shooting.*
>
> Q. *Started pushing them into a ravine?*
>
> *Off into the ravine. It was a ditch. And so we started pushing them off, and we started shooting them, so all together we just pushed them all off, and just started using automatics on them. And then . . .*
>
> Q. *Again— men, women, and children?*
>
> *Men, women, and children.*
>
> Q. *And babies?*
>
> *And babies.*[17]

My warning is this. We are "set up" for authorities by our early training in conformity and by our unwillingness to stand up and rock the boat, when it is easier to go along. Being close to the one giving the orders—in the same room or group—makes it more difficult.[18] Yet if we are to be free, politically, and humane, we must listen to our voices and be unwilling to stay silent on those occasions when we see something wrong happening and the crowd wants to go along. This is preaching by me, of course. But the whole point of social knowledge is to increase your ability to speak up, and to live more effectively and humanely. The sociological study of power relationships and authority, just touched on here, is a beginning.

Relationships involve more than power and authority, more than roles and their definition. They are set into history. *When* a relationship is set up it will have a major effect on *what* that relationship can be. It is to this historical dimension of relationships and to the topic of the family and the life cycle in history, that we now turn.

Age Relationships: A Historical Approach

An inspection of our own American past can give us an idea of the many ways in which the relationships people have at particular points in their life cycle change, along with the social context within which they are set, as history moves on. We can see how social forces over the centuries affect the family—the social form in which the stages take place. Each of these age relationships have a place in family life, though not all are lived in the bosom of the family in all periods in history. Our study will provide us with a preliminary insight into changes in the basic meaning of the family from the past to the present—the meaning to the people at the time they are living. Perhaps we can even get some idea of what the life-cycle stages, and our family relationships, might be like in the future. Let's look at changes in the meaning and nature of relationships at three key periods of life: childhood, adolescence, and old age.

Childhood and the Family: Medieval Europe to Modern America

Philippe Aries has investigated the life cycle from the Middle Ages to the present, with special attention to the period we now call childhood. In the Middle Ages, he found that a clearly marked period with that name was *missing*. After a long presentation of the evidence, he concluded:

> In medieval society the idea of childhood did not exist; this is not to suggest that children were neglected, forsaken, or despised. The idea of childhood is not to be confused with affection for children: it corresponds to an awareness of the particular nature of childhood, that particular

nature which distinguishes the child from the adult, even the young adult. In medieval society this awareness was lacking. That is why, as soon as the child could live without the constant solicitude of his mother, his nanny or his cradle-rocker, he belonged to adult society.[19]

The birth of the modern world in Europe is reflected in the move away from this concept of the child as a small adult. In the 1600s and early 1700s the new idea developed that childhood is a social stage, that children belong in a category, and that each family as a *unit* is responsible for the moral education of the child. Schools began to have a role now. Aries also finds that schools and colleges, where they existed, did not at this time demand that all children of a certain age be in a certain grade in school the way we tend to. The Enlightenment, however, did mean the *consideration* of the topic of children, as children.

The modern "nuclear" or core family—the arrangement of father, mother, and young children typical of our recent past—was in many ways an invention of the Enlightenment in Europe. But because America lagged behind Europe at first, until about 1750 or so, in the American colonies a different and earlier European-style arrangement was common. Children were kept at home until the age of seven. Then an exchange occurred. Parents lent out a child as a part-servant, part-apprentice to another family they knew. In return, they often accepted another family's child. The theory was that manners, social responsibility, and a trade were better taught away from home by people who might not be as soft and forgiving as one's own parents. Family membership, for the middle classes, meant the ownership of a house, the family heirlooms, and a family name, but relations between parents and children were not *expected* to be close.

The major event that changed all this was the invention of formal schooling for children, in the 1600's and early 1700's in Europe and later, after 1750 in most parts of the American colonies. Schooling-as against going out into the world very young in the semi-servant arrangment—was invented because of new theories about people, theories that proposed that human nature could be improved by moral teaching in schools. The increasing desire of parents to have their own children at home when they were young was another factor. Thus we find that in the first American century, from 1650 to 1750, much lending-out of children occurs, but from about 1750 on, the family and the grammar school as we know them today begin to become a real feature on the social landscape. Still, several major differences between then and now are important. First, the death rate of infants and small children was much higher then. More than half the children born in the early years of the American experiment didn't live to see their tenth birthday. This did not, I think, lessen the grief of parents at the loss of children. But life was hard and it did not lead to the kind of long-term stability and sense of permanence of the parent-child relationship that we expect today.[20] Many parents had children one right after another, at least in part because parents were aware that a large number would not survive to adulthood. Children were also additional manpower for the family farm, and valued for it.

A second, related difference from today lay in the shortness of life of the parents themselves. The dangers of repeated childbirth under primitive living conditions meant a high death rate for women. The average age of men, at death, was also considerably younger than it is today. Thus in these early years the instability of the family, with children, mothers and fathers here today and gone tomorrow, plus the custom of boarding-out children at seven or so, led the core family of today to be less common. It was only when we arrived at the period after the American revolution, the period from the 1780's to the mid-1800s, that the family form we know today first began to be possible. For only in this era does one find the children beginning to stay home and going to grammar school. In the East, the greater degree of settled community life and some improvements in public health led for the first time to a lowering in the death rate of children and adults. The "empty nest" of today—two parents with grown children moved away—was a rarity, for at least one child usually outlived one of the parents.

In Chapter 1 I discussed under the topic of women's self-image, the changes in women's role brought about by the industrial revolution. The ideal of the mother-father-child family that had been a middle-class norm for almost a century began at that time, but not even then could it become the reality for the *working class,* where both parents have always had to work. But today the middle class may finally be joining the working class, as to family forms. By the late 1970s, because of the rising cost of living with its cost squeeze on households, far more mothers with children were working than not, middle class as well as blue collar, and the new norm may very well be two working parents. In addition, a new valuing of singleness as an "alternate ideal" instead of a curse, more social approval of marriage without children and greater acceptance of divorce have added new factors to the equation, which directly affect the quality, nature, course, and experience of childhood.

Thus environmental factors both physical and economic, have a direct impact on what kind of family is possible. But one steady theme does stand out from era to era. Children have been increasingly valued outwardly and openly as time has passed, and the outward and open expression of affection toward them has grown as well. What is ironic about this longest of trends is that recent developments may include a drastic downturn in the birth rate. But even this may pass, due to yet further changes in the social and economic environment. Childhood, like any other stage in the life cycle, is a hostage to its time and place.

The Invention of Adolescence

Long-term changes in the nature of schooling and the development of a stable core family sometime after 1850 brought other changes. No social reformer works in a vacuum; changes can only occur in a society almost ready for them. In America some historians have concluded that the beginning of our present century was the time when a new life-cycle stage was first consciously described, even though it had been in process of un-noticed gradual development for more than a century. This new stage in life was called *adolescence.* Here is historian Joseph Kett on its emergence:

> Between 1900 and 1920 both the concepts and institutions which have dominated youth work for the last half century took shape, almost final shape. G. Stanley Hall's *Adolescence,* published in 1904, was the seminal book, but direct radiations from Hall's work formed just one element in the process. All sorts of individuals—earnest humanitarian reformers, boys-workers, nervous parents, school bureaucrats, and academicians— stumbled onto the study of adolescence after 1900, sometimes drawing inspiration from Hall, sometimes not. But no sooner had they converged than they parted company, going off in separate directions and to new interests. They left young people holding the bag, so to speak, for the institutions created in the early 20th century survived to become an enduring form of custody for youth long after the ideas and impulses which created them were laid to rest.[21]

How can we explain this creation of an age category and the consequences it has had for the relationships that people in the category have with their families and each other? How can we explain the complimentary new idea of "adult society"—something these young now are defined as not belonging to?

Three historical periods are natural dividing lines in looking at all this—the period just after our Revolution to the mid-1800s, or the industrial revolution; this time to the turn of the century; and 1900 to the present.

A revolution always leaves its mark on the social process afterward. America, as a new country, was a country undergoing changes in opportunity for careers. In the post-Revolutionary period one carryover from an earlier era was the mixing of youth from different backgrounds and ages in a fluid and flexible class system. For one thing, the ages of youth in school varied a great deal. Academies (private prep schools or junior colleges) enrolled thirteen-year-old ministers' sons along with twenty-two-year-old farmers' sons. The few colleges around such as Harvard, were actually quite rough and rowdy institutions, dangerous to students and faculty alike.[22]

Again, the boarding-out system of the Middle Ages could still be found in the early years of the new American nation, although more children were kept at home till eleven, twelve, or thirteen:

> Leaving home was ... an experience common to youth of different classes, although its nature differed from class to class. Landowning farmers sanctioned seasonal departures of sons from home, but wanted their children back in the spring and summer. Wealthy merchants often sent their sons out as cabin boys at 8 or 9 or as supercargo [sailing apprentice] at 15 or 16 as part of a process of grooming that was to lead to a junior partnership at 21. Differences between rich and poor were often those of motive rather than deed; children of the wealthy left home because of parental preference rather than stark necessity.[23]

The second period, from about 1850 to the turn of the present century, marked the real fork in the road between poor and working-class youth on the one hand and upper and professional class youth on the other. As the average educational level began to rise and as new opportunities began to open in the worlds of industry and business, the upper and professional classes pushed for longer years of education for their children—high school and college—to guarantee them the best chance at the new jobs. In contrast there was terrible poverty among small farmers and immigrants from Europe in the growing cities. This pushed their children out of school quickly and into new lives as members of a growing army of low-paid and ill-housed industrial workers. Youth became a class-based experience.[24]

After the beginning of the present century public high school education increased and social reformers had real successes in their campaign against child labor in factories. One result was that more and more youth at all class levels stayed in school into their middle and late teens. This new period created by the school experience then became the target of conceptualizers and the idea of adolescence was born. By the midpoint of our century it had come to mean for many enforced school, no job opportunity, and dependence upon one's parents. The period has now lengthened almost ten years more for many young people because of the unemployment of post high school and postcollege youth. Living arrangements that in early colonial times ended at the age of seven or eight are today carried on into the twenties.

The Politics of Aging: Puritan to Gray Panther

A revolution is always based on a change in attitudes toward authority. In Puritan America, from 1630 to 1700, the old, especially the wealthy and middle-class old, were powerful and respected. But there has been a profound revolution in values, as David Fischer puts it, "Both young and old have greatly changed their attitudes toward one another, and their expectations for themselves as well. The people of early America exalted old age; their descendants have made a cult of youth."[25]

In Puritan times and part of the century after them, the oldest wealthy citizens of each community were at the top of the power and prestige hierarchy. For example, in the Meeting—the Sunday meeting hall that was both town hall and church—the oldest citizens were given the best seats. This pattern of "dignifying the seats" according to age lasted in many New England towns until the late 1700s. Also, the stylish ages were the older ones. Fashions, such as the powdered wig and the cut of men's clothes, tended to stress the stylishness of the seniors. When people lied about their age, they systematically added a few years rather than subtracting them. Far more unflattering words were commonly used to describe the young than were applied to the old. Most important of all in an agricultural society, the man of the house did not give his land to his children, but required them to live in separate houses on the land, often until the old man died. The adult children may have resented this, but his authority was unquestioned, resting as it did on an economic base as well as social values and laws that protected his prestige and rights.[26]

Two long-term trends worked to unseat the old from this power position. First, as America industrialized, the economic power of landholding dropped away. Children who now had another way to make a living in factories did not have to stay on the farm, in a dependent status, on into their thirties and forties. The second factor was a change in overall political ideology which actually began almost thirty years before America declared independence from Britain. The new ideology said, "Down with *old*, illegitimate traditional power" (the King of England). It questioned the right of any political body to rule by simple extension of tradition. And as the new, anti-traditional way of thinking came in, the earlier worship of the old began to go out of fashion. So did the older style of clothing, especially knee breeches. A new post-Revolutionary generation passed the first laws forcing retirement at a certain age. There were slow changes in town government, leading eventually to the disappearance of the custom of seating people by age. Fashions favored the young woman as well as men and new swear words were invented to describe the "useless" old—"codger," "geezer". The customs began to change, and the old lost their grip on the young.[27]

By the late 1800s the modern industrial era, had replaced the older world I have described. The old were becoming a social problem. Yet it would be the 1930s before laws were passed creating the American Social Security system, and even this was, and is, pitiful by European standards. From 1900 on, unemployment was high enough in most times to make it difficult for those *under* sixty-five to find work, so the rest of the population organized against the old. And modern medicine was having the effect that more and more people survived to enter the unwanted ranks of the old. The present era has a higher proportion of older people in it than any previous era, and the proportion is still growing. The situation became almost the reverse of the situation two centuries ago. The elderly of today's upper classes can hold the next generation ransom in terms of wills—a power similar to the old Puritan's hold on land. More and more of the rest of the old are scorned and rejected. Their children and the whole economy have relegated them to the social scrap heap.

Yet the activities of every new era grow in reaction to the previous one. Having been thrown together onto a collective scrap heap, the present generation of older Americans, using their talent, know-how and in many ways their high reserves of energy, are organizing to become a permanent political group. They are fighting against real estate tax laws that drive them out their homes—homes they have paid off but cannot hold on to under Social Security funds. They are fighting for better health care, and even against the economic system that has discarded them at age 65. In the years to come they may become one of our most important forces for social *change,* rather than preservers of tradition. The retirement laws themselves are under attack by the Gray Panthers and other national organizations of older Americans.[28] Not all old people are out there working for change, of course—probably only a minority. But enough are to remind us that the action of the "new old" is set, as a life cycle stage, into a given historical period, and it makes a difference what period it is.

Childhood, Adolescence, Old Age: Some Common Themes

One of the simple observations I like to make about society, for new students in sociology, is that "The leg bone is connected to the knee bone." Note how impossible it was for us to talk about childhood as a stage without talking about parents, and how difficult if not irrelevant it is to talk about the birth of adolescence without understanding the role of schools and the new industrial era. Each stage of the life cycle, and place in the network of family relationships, stands related to the other elements in the sociological institution of the family at one point in time. That's the first common theme. The second is closely related to the first—when one element changes, the others must change as well—the knee bone is connected to the leg bone. So when, in history in our nation, the industrial revolution comes, it creates a new set of problems and opportunities which are reflected at each stage of the life cycle. The farms lose their power to industry and the old in control of those farms lose their power over the young. Growth in the bureaucratic order—the routine of factory and school—leads to the more precise categorizing of people and the creation of adolescence. But the very presence of older children in the home is itself the result of historical changes, and these changes affect all the members of the family, all the stages of the life cycle, and the whole network of family relationships.

What the historical viewpoint can give us, in other words, is help with one of the most important insights of the sociological approach —that there really *is* a system out there. Learning how it operates demands not only snapshots of social arrangements at present, but also an understanding of how changes in one stage in the life cycle are produced and cause other changes in turn. But what does all of this new investigation of relationships mean for you? We now turn to this question, in concluding our brief exploration of the sociology of relationships.

Relationships: Compulsion Versus Choice

Medical students sometimes develop a malady known as "medical students' disease." Seeing all of the possible illnesses people can get they develop a supersensitivity to every nuance and twinge of their own bodies, and become temporary hypochondriacs. Another version of this problem, common at college, is the roommate who is taking abnormal psychology, and who persists in giving every statement you make a label, or a disease. Whatever else, I hope this introduction into some of the dimensions and issues of human relationships does not have the same effect. Sociology cannot be useful as a cure-all for your personal troubles, nor can it be used very constructively to find labels to paste on the relationships you have experienced or plan to experience. Rather, it is a type of sensitizer to the complexities of the many kinds of relationships that exist between people. A sociological view can help you point out the unnoticed, question the unquestioned, and, above all, give an idea of what is *possible.*

There can be a personal payoff from the long-term sociological study of relationships in the area of compulsion versus choice. To the extent that we are unaware of factors affecting our relations with others, we can wind up as the prisoner of the past, obeying compulsions and constrictions that may have made sense at some other time but at present only serve to enrich some people or make some people happy at the expense of a lot of others. Take the structure of relationships—the dyad, the triangle, and so on. A sociological perspective that includes awareness of these forms will certainly help in understanding the why of some things found in relationships. And the whys may aid with the solution of a problem in a relationship—or even the decision to endure the difficulty.

Roles are changing around us, and the hue and cry from each social group that has experienced oppression and cruelty is rising every day. One temptation is to wish that some of the confrontation and chaos would go away. For if women, old people, blacks, and homosexuals are going to change their ideas of themselves, that is inevitably going to change the way they act toward me and the ways they are going to expect me to act toward them To react by pulling the emergency cord—demanding it all stop—is not going to work. Being happy about all of it is probably not a real option either. Most of us have become accustomed to things as they are, and things feel comfortable that way. Yet sociology can act as a guide helping us to see that the roles and relationships we once thought were the only right ones are in fact only a few among many possibilities—and that other people have the right to their own arrangements. Sociology won't necessarily convert us all to activists, but at least it can show us why the goals some activists are pushing for make sense to them. And maybe, with a little thought, the goals will come to make sense to us as well.

As for the power dimension in relationships, no sociologist will ever be able to lift the moral burden off your shoulders. Sociology cannot tell you if or when a particular power arrangement—between yourself and someone else or between yourself and a government—should be overthrown. It can, however, remind you that there *is* an issue here, a critical one. Obedience in power relationships, unquestioning obedience, heads us down the path to ruin. In the words of the old saying, "All that is necessary for evil to triumph is for good men to do nothing." On the other hand, sociological analyses of authority do not usually counsel anarchy either—the disruption of one set of power relationships with no plan to replace them with another set. In politics the usual sequel to anarchy, the usual result, is a totalitarian state imposed from above to keep order. But no matter how you work out your own views on such issues, a study of power relations and of the leader-follower issue in all its variety from local politics to presidents, from bosses to gurus, cannot help but give you a greater sense of what is going on. It can also help you learn where to draw the line, if necessary.

Finally, the sociological perspective, especially on including history, can give you a far better grasp of the miserably alienated and broken relationships that are far too common between the generations. An appreciation of others' point of view—brotherhood and sisterhood and humanhood across the age levels—is one of the most important items on any agenda for social action. Who and what has contributed to making our lock-step, locked-in life-cycle, and helped to create its present wastebasket end? A sociological inspection of the family in history, and at the present time, can give you the background to act in ways that can constructively change the present situation. There are forces and interests that will be threatened by these attempts, and they will fight back. No question about it—to gain a greater degree of control over the destiny of our relationships is a giant, and a lifelong task. Perhaps some sociology can help.

For Further Reading

Georg Simmel. *The Sociology of Georg Simmel.* Translated and edited by Kurt Wolff. New York: Free Press, 1964.
 Not easy reading, but worth it. Divided into short essays and manageable sections on almost any topic involving relationships you might imagine. The classic geometric sociology of human bonds.
Edward T. Hall. *The Silent Language.* Garden City, N.Y.:Doubleday, 1959.
 An excellent introduction to the nonword dimensions of communication by an anthropologist and linguist. An especially interesting topic Hall discusses is the customs that different cultures have for dealing with the relationships between people in the face-to-face situation.
Theodore Mills. *Small Groups.* Englewood Cliffs, N.J.: Prentice-Hall, 1970.
 A brief but thorough summary on small-group research. It starts with the early pioneers like Lewin, Bales, and Miles, then goes on to more recent developments. Written by a specialist for beginning students.
Erving Goffman. *The Presentation of Self in Everyday life.* Garden City, N.Y.: Doubleday, 1959.
 A colorful and thorough discussion, with many examples, of the ways in which we try to manage our appearances and other peoples perception of who we are. Goffman is cynical, but the book is well worth investigating.
Scott Turow. *One L.* Baltimore: Penguin, 1977.
 A first-person account of the first year at Harvard Law School, including the pain of the experience, written by a former writing instructor who decided he wanted to become a lawyer.

Stanley Milgram. *Obedience to Authority.* New York: Harper and Row, 1975.
The complete record of a terrifying series of experiments on obedience
carried out by Milgram. Clearly written and of extreme importance: the
power dimension to relationships as seen from peoples' own interpretations of them.

Philippe Aries. *Centuries of Childhood: A Social History of Family Life,* translated by Roger Baldick (New York: Vintage Books, 1963).
The development of the idea of childhood wasn't possible until families
started to hang onto their children and build schools to educate them close
to home. This book discusses families and childhood over 400 years.
Scholarly and detailed, but very brilliant and entertaining.

Joseph F. Kett. *Rites of Passage: Adolescence in America 1790 to the Present.*
New York: Basic Books, 1977.
The invention of adolescence is a factor determined by the growth of
modern, industrial, bureaucratic America. Historical perspective is given
on the growth of the child-serving professions. Social history, sociology,
and critique of present-day America, in one good book.

David Hackett Fischer. *Growing Old in America.* New York: Oxford University Press, 1976.
This work discusses old age in America from Puritan times to the present.
Amazing parallels in the work of Fischer and Kett make it a good idea to
read the two together to get a real grasp of what the life cycle was like in
Puritan times, early colonial times, the mid-1800s and at the turn of the
century. Short, scholarly, clearly written.

Edward Shorter. *The Making of the Modern Family.* New York: Basic, 1975.
An approach to the family as a unit, going over the same ground as Aries,
Kett, and Fischer. Shorter, a sociologist with an interest in history, adds
yet another piece to the puzzle. Higly recommended and controversial
within sociology today.

Deborah David and Robert Brannon (editors). *The Forty-nine Per Cent Majority: The Male Sex Role.* Reading, Mass: Addison-Wesley, 1976.
A reader on the male sex role in modern America. A novel way to get into
the issues of changing sex roles as they are related to one another.

Chapter

THREE
Finding Work

Bob and Ray, the radio comedians, usually signed off the air like this: Bob would say, "Until next week—hang by your thumbs. . . ." Ray would cheerily add, "And write if you get work!" Somehow the humor has gone out of this. For too many people today, finding work *at all* is a most uncheerful prospect. Almost as bad, for many, is the work they actually find when they are successful in their search.

Sociologists have long been involved in the study of work, careers, and occupational and professional groups, as well as deeply concerned with the social position people arrive at as a consequence of the kind of work they do.

Several areas in sociology are rapidly developing a fund of knowledge that is both interesting and important in dealing with the problems of work in our time. I will begin by introducing the sociological perspective on the ways people become involved with one another in entering the world of work. Then we will consider the broader question, Who has opportunity for advancement and who doesn't? Then we will take up special issue of women's work, a focus for much recent research. The place of work, especially the large organizations in which many of us work, is a major focus for sociological studies, and we will consider it also. Finally, what needs to be done to change some of the realities of work, and how may this action involve you?

Together, these approaches will constitute a brief review of the ways in which sociologists watch us earn the money to pay the rent.

The Journey Toward Work

Choosing a job is a new idea on the stage of history.[1] For most of man's life on earth, the demands of climate and survival and the rule of custom dictated that people would work at the same tasks as their parents before them, and that sons and daughters would follow the traditions to the end of time. Yet as far back as we have historical records there is evidence of some specialization. Even in a fishing society there were canoe builders as well as a large group of fishermen; yet specialization was exceptional and perhaps one or two men specialized in making nets.

Emile Durkheim was fascinated with the division of labor in modern society as this contrasts with work in non-Western, non-technological societies. He noted that one of the most important characterisitics of modern society was specialization—a thousand specific occupations, each with its own skills, all necessary to keep the ball rolling.[2] Specialization has become such a powerful thing that a few years ago, for example, fifteen drawbridge operators were able to paralyze New York City by putting all the highway bridges up and hiding the keys![3]

In this specialized modern world of work, career choices are made or at least can be made, by individuals. How this choice process takes place and how it fits remarkably closely with the needs for occupants of the existing job slots in the society constitute a problem of great interest to sociologists. The trail through school, into the different worlds of work, and for some into the special world of the professions, has been followed in detail.

In Chapter 1 I discussed how middle- and upper-class children tend to fit in and succeed in our American schools from the very beginning. In many cases this experience leads to the pencil-and-paper world of high school and post-high school training. By contrast, the class-biased educational experience of poor and working-class children often leads to an early feeling of inadequacy in this pencil-and-paper world and an early choice in favor of the "vocational" or "vocational-technical" or "office-secretarial" track in high school. The status system of public education quickly descends on young people, whether they are in the "lower" or "voc" track or are headed for college. And for every "voc-tech" palace with modern, European- style standards and the latest training in electronics there are a hundred educational dumping grounds with poor and disgruntled teachers, obsolete equipment, and delinquent students, all guaranteeing a disrupted and disciplinary atmosphere.[4]

Two research interviewers, Aaron Cicourel and John Kitsuse, did a classic depth analysis of a key fork in the road to a career—the point where students meet the guidance counselors in junior high schools. They found that these counselors in addition to doing a certain amount of plain prying and amateur psychiatry, were mainly occupied with making sure that most youth did not develop hopes of reaching job positions too different from those of their parents.[5] They had the main leverage in telling children and their parents whether the children should try for the college track or pick one of the others. When probed for reasons why they advised one or the other course of study, the answers they gave to the sociologists ultimately boiled down to the counselors' estimate of the amount of money the parents had for education. For example, if an eighth-grader was a C student and wasn't trying but was the son of the town surgeon, he was urged to get the grades up to join the college track in the ninth grade. In the case of the son of a carpenter, the same behavior led to the recommendation of trade school and would often find support at home. The process can be more subtle, but the gradual lowering of students sights, plus the known insecurities of the job market for college graduates, leads inevitably to the repetition of career tracks from one generation to the next.

But what about the public two-year community colleges? Aren't they "second chance" institutions for a lot of students who did poorly in high school or were miscounseled? Yes, to some extent this is so. But, in an extensive study of American higher education, Christopher Jencks and David Riesman found that this "second chance" idea tends to be an illusion. Close inspection of the courses offered in most community colleges will show that a good number, anywhere from a half to three-quarters, are actually occupational training for low-level secretarial, technical, and office work. They are almost a repeat of the noncollege tracks in high school and often do *not* provide second chances. Sociologically speaking, they function as a kind of program of final vocational training. They provide the feel of college, with sometimes even a pretty campus, but not the occupational and career payoffs. They function to let down gradually the aspirations of those who for a variety of reasons could not attend a four-year school but don't want to think that it's all over at high school graduation. Of course evening degree programs in college are growing, even liberal arts programs, so the chance never completely disappears.[6]

I have been falling informally into the use of the word "career." But it is important to be clear and precise about how this word is used sociologically. First, there is the issue of the difference between a career and a *job.* Second, the problem of shape of careers, and the question of who does the shaping. Third, there's the problem of observing careers as they develop. New approaches have been developed by sociologists interested in seeing these differences and problems at first hand. We can touch on this growing field of research next, for studying careers can be an aid to developing one for yourself.

Learning the Ropes: Medical Schools and Skyscrapers

Let's begin by defining *career*: a sequence of jobs with increasing responsibility, in which the skills and experience of previous jobs build and add to the value, both personal and economic, of the present one. A career has a socially defined pattern related to the field of work, the job opportunities of the society, and the skills of the individual. A career is built in stages, and not all people have careers. Most, in fact, have instead a series of jobs that only vaguely relate one to the next. The reason for the difference lies in the importance of customs and culture at work, as this affects jobs but especially long-term vocational commitments in careers. Yet for all jobs, an *occupational culture* exists—a set of folkways gathered around the job that must be learned along with the work itself. This is true whether or not the job is part of a defined career sequence—whether one is doing the work a first-year medical student does or simple work on the floor of a department store. Everett Hughes, one of sociology's keenest observers of people at work, commented on this:

> Especially when an occupation develops its own institution for control of the occupation, and protection of its prerogatives, it is likely to develop what we may call a culture, an etiquette, and a group within which one

may attain the satisfaction of his wishes. This etiquette may be more or less incomprehensible to the outside, or lay, world.[7]

Sociologists have been exploring this critical phase of initiation to work—especially sociologists whose research technique includes note-taking, interviews in the field and participant observation in a sidelines role on the scene. And because both kinds of work have now been observed, it is possible to compare initiation into a traditional profession—medicine, for example—and initiation into a craft or even an ordinary job. Howard Becker, Blanche Geer, Everett Hughes, and Anselm Strauss spent a year in medical school, going to classes and eating with students, staying up at night with them in dorms and hospital wards, observing them learning their profession.[8] They soon found that the students' view of the profession was rather different from the faculty's. The stress on learning so much material so fast meant that the students had to evolve ways of defending themselves against overwork. They set standards of how much work they would be willing to do. A student perspective was developed— the student group gradually developed a fairly united attitude toward their work situation, along with a set of values and ways of acting in this situation. In the first year—primarily in classes and laboratory work—the student perspective was summed up by the phrase "You can't do it all":

1. In spite of all our efforts, we cannot learn everything in the time available.
2. We will work just as hard as ever, but now we will study in only the most effective and economical ways, and learn only the things that are important.
3. Some students said: We will decide whether something is important according to whether it is important in medical practice. Other students said: We will decide whether something is important according to whether it is what the faculty wants us to know.[9]

When the research team observed students in the last two clinical and hospital training years in medical school, they found that new perspectives were developed in the new settings. The student's attitudes toward their work got more closely related to choices of specialties. Group stereotypes were developed about "the surgeon's work" and "the general practitioner's work," and these affected actual choices. Becker and Geer, two members of the study team, published an article on what they called "the fate of idealism in medical school." This study, done in the fifties, found students in the first two years beginning with ideas about mastering all of medical knowledge. Their experiences led them to drop the ideal and to develop instead the more manageable goal of mastering a specialty.[10] An interesting note: no questions were asked by this otherwise inquisitive team about the money issue. This must have been important as a motive then, and it certainly has been recently. For example, studies in the mid-seventies found an overwhelming majority of medical students choosing the career initially not for intellectual motives or to help make the society a better one, but because of the two advantages of job security and high income.

A comparison can be made to the occupational culture of a nonprofessional group. Geer trained another generation of field observers. As graduate students each picked a nonprofessional occupation to research. Most of these people training for occupations —butcher's helpers, students in barber school, and so on—called their on-the-job training "learning the ropes" or otherwise indicated that indeed informal learning was going on.[11] What was fascinating to the researchers was that Hughes' observations were borne out here as well. High-steel workers, for example, had an occupational culture of bravado. There was much "macho" swearing and testing of one another's "cool" in response to joking insults. This process of testing a high-steel apprentice was called "binging" by the sociologist who observed it, and it had a function in that job setting:

> Workers use binging to test trustworthiness and self-control. Will a man keep his cool under blistering personal attacks? If he loses his poise, it indicates he may lose control in other threatening situations-e.g., high above the ground. If he takes such kidding seriously, he may carry a grudge into a situation where vengeance is easy.[12]

Both the medical student study and the high-steel-worker study were done by people who worked alongside their subjects (taking notes on the high steel girders in the case of the second study). Being with your subject is a characteristic of this style of studying the sociology of work. There are others of equal importance—for example, quantitative studies. To know the statistics on discrimination and the job market is extremely important for getting an idea of the opportunity picture. The importance of the more intimate style of research on work lies in being close enough to the people and spending enough time with them to see things as they do. In addition to the general idea we can get about work cultures, this style allows us to explore the realities of work experience and its implications for career advancement, depending on the degree to which you fit the occupational culture or change it to fit you.

The Politics of Skill

Occupations are groups—groups organized to defend themselves against outside intervention as well as organized to advance the economic interests of the occupation's members.[13] On the other hand, occupations can have subgroups that act on behalf of consumers.[14] Let's take up these situations in turn.

Action to protect buddies at work can be a cause for joy or a cause for grief, depending on whether you are defined by your work mates as a buddy. How would women come through the high-steel worker's binging routine, given the macho nature of binging and the fact that the steel workers' language is full of obscene statements about women? From medical students to butcher's apprentices, work can have prejudices and attitudes that make the work setting a most exclusive place and make true career opportunities there a closed book for many people. Second, occupational groups can defend what they are doing from outside inspection. Marsha Millman recently gave us a good example of this from her field work. She studied a group of surgeons in a community hospital.[15] She found they were quite successful in resisting any controls over their work, claiming "medical expertise." But, she notes, they were often motivated by a combination of greed and egotism. What they had in common, she says, was a code of silence, a code not too dissimilar from that of the Mafia:

> As doctors increasingly feel abused, persecuted, insufficiently appreciated, and misunderstood by their patients and the public, they are closing ranks more tightly than ever. As one department chief explained: "I don't believe patients should be told when they've acquired an iatrogenic [physician-produced] illness. They just can't understand the risks of the procedures we do, so why should we tell them when they've become sick from something we've tried? So they can sue us?"[16]

The U.S. Department of Health, Education, and Welfare, (HEW) has programs that are attempting to penetrate walls of secrecy to assess more efficiently whether, for example, surgeons are doing too much surgery. But what Elliot Freidson calls "professional dominance"—doctor's professional control over other health occupations and people's belief in doctor expertise—gives doctors freedom to cause damage and not have to answer for it.[17] Sociologists often function as bell ringers to the world in situations of this kind, opening new fields to public scrutiny. Not everyone agrees with what the sociologists bring forth, of course. Millman got into a heated argument over the issue of coverups by doctors with a representative of the American Medical Association, who defended the profession, on a morning discussion of her book on the NBC *Today* Show. Regardless of the outcome of that debate, no study means no issue in the first place.

Not all occupational-group action is as selfish as that observed above. For example, other sociologists have been deeply interested in the new phenomenon of people who have become activist professionals such as the physicians in the Medical Committee for Human Rights and the lawyer volunteers who have worked with the activist Ralph Nader.[18] By analyzing their activities and writing of their struggle, a new generation of workers can begin to critically evaluate where their own newly chosen occupation stands on issues such as consumer rights, democratic action[18] and giving people fair value for work performed. Some sociologists have actively joined such work-related activist organizations. These sociologists have helped develop the data and the social analyses to challenge, for example, corporations' handling of occupational disease on the workplace and the treatment of the black and the poor in city hospitals. They have supplied data on and analyses of the human and social consequences of refusing abortions to those who need them and can't pay. In these ways and many more, sociologists are taking a hand in political action about work and social life in general.

The analysis of job experience and occupational culture is just one way of looking at work sociologically. It is also important to see how work and occupations fit into the overall social system, to understand the opportunity of individuals as part of the picture of the wider society within which they are set. The nature of opportunity, of equality, of social hierarchy and social mobility—of individuals and groups— is of central importance. This is our second way of looking at work, to which we now turn.

Does Opportunity Knock at All?

A large number of Americans seem to accept the idea that our society is primarily set up as a place where people race for success, and that this is a fine arrangement. To the winners go the spoils. To the losers —well, "They get what they deserve." The sociological point of view operates differently. Questions are asked. What is *opportunity*, and what is meant by *equality*? Is *equality* the same thing as *equality of opportunity*? How well has each generation done in comparison with the previous one? Have we all been climbing slightly on the social ladder in comparison with our parents, and what is this "climbing" anyway? Some people seem more successful than others. Who is successful and who isn't and why? Are the differences due to innate ability, to racism and the other isms, to schooling, to the job market? Finally, what is to be done about all this?

Equality and Opportunity: The Debate

One of the classic arguments among America's founding fathers was over how seriously the new United States was going to take its own Revolutionary slogans about equality and democracy now that the war was over and the British had gone home.[19] None of them was pushing for the right to vote for every American, including women and poor people. But Thomas Jefferson was willing to write a Constitution that would let a lot more people participate in government than Alexander Hamilton was. None of the fathers was in favor of letting slaves go free. The whole history of our nation, in the areas of equality and opportunity, has been that of a long and sometimes bloody struggle, which is by no means over. The poor and powerless have struggled for more opportunity and equality against a well-organized, powerful minority and against a background of a generally disinterested majority of citizens.[20] In the early years a land-owning aristocracy was the dominant element in the powerful minority, then a merchant-capitalist class, and then, after the mid-1800s, the giant corporations. These corporations' decisions, given power by their great control over the economy, have shaped opportunity or lack of it for millions. And this power lasts. But again, what do we mean by equality and opportunity?

Equality is an absolute, a goal, an ideal. It means total parity and similar reward for men and women, for black and white. It means, in short, everyone at the same level. Think about this. First, as far as we can go back in Western history, to the Middle Ages, such a world has never existed. Second, look into your own heart and think. To what extent are you presently prepared to give away what you have, or what your parents have, in order to award it to others who have less than you? If you begin to balk a little at this idea, it is hardly surprising. Since infancy you probably have been brought up to believe that any and all of your possessions are sacred, and you have a sacred right to hang on to them—all of them. AND NOBODY IS GOING TO TAKE ANY OF IT AWAY! Precisely.

Yet think a minute about what would have to happen for the goal of equality to be reached. Those of great wealth think that way too, and unquestionably the economic system that had piled it up would have to be changed. This brings fear and uncertainty to many people and not just the rich. For the indoctrination many people have received through their lifetime suggests that either hopeless resignation to the present, or violent revolution, are the only alternatives available. Indoctrination, subtle but real, also suggests that a rigidly controlled society like the Soviet Union, with its prison camps for political dissenters, is the only alternative we have to the present situation.[21] In addition to fear of the byproducts of trying to make a change, most people's belief that they are *legitimately* winning or losing at the present race for income and jobs ignores the obvious fact that we don't all start equal. In general, those behind strive for equality, most of those ahead have a tendency to protect what they have. Thus the stalemate-the majority desiring a better lot in life but afraid of change and as yet not organized to bring it about, with a powerful and well-organized minority fighting against any major change that might affect their interests.

Opportunity—what is it? The classic American image is that of the Statue of Liberty, offering a chance in a new land to the millions of Americans who came here from elsewhere. But what does this chance mean, anyway? Is it the same as equality? No. It is usually understood to mean the chance not only to become equal with others but to surpass them, to become rich or famous or both. Obviously then, if we are going to be logical about it , unless everyone is going to wind up equal, the opportunity taken by some will be lost by others (unless we change the rules completely, and have a different kind of economy). How is opportunity to be defined? Do we mean an equal chance for a high school and a college education? An equal chance to read the want ads and pound the pavements? A government-paid, non-dead-end government job, if the private sector doesn't have any openings? And what about the long run? Is my opportunity to get raises and book royalties the same as that of a clerk at Sears? Who will decide who gets more opportunity, or less? Regardless of how we define it? If we go on fighting for it at present, is it a fair fight? When we look at the fine print of the word "opportunity" we see immediately that it usually does *not* mean the same thing as equality.

What then of *equality of opportunity*, the legal phrase that we have been hearing for almost thirty years, as a consequence of Supreme Court decisions, laws in education, and antidiscrimination clauses in other laws? To begin with, note that the phrase does not mean actual equality is going to result. My equal opportunity to get a job, when matched up against your equal opportunity to get the same job, can still mean that I get it and you don't. We both had an equal chance, and you lost. In the 1960s, it was widely believed that just equalizing the chances for success would be enough to make this a society of equals. Some still believe this. Others felt and still feel that opportunity in a situation where those with most of the jobs and most of the power are still controlling the situation is not really even opportunity, that the word is empty. They ask instead for a head start, extra help, special treatment, in order to make up for years, even centuries, of past prejudice and lack of opportunity. Government programs for women and for blacks, to name two groups, often attempt to change the present setup in this manner. But note—this is actually "compensatory," or extra, opportunity, not just equal opportunity, and to the extent that others lose opportunity as these groups gain it, they can be expected to complain and to exert political pressure to stop the programs. The Bakke case on "reverse discrimination," with a white student suing a medical school for his non-admission while admitting blacks because of a quota favoring some of them, is a well-known case of this type at present. By the way, working to prevent increasing the opportunitues for minorities can count on a general fund of resentment from the millions of other Americans who have been told, by their incomes and their likely future, that they have already lost any race for success they have entered.[22]

The position of the sociologist is controversial here, for he or she must describe the situation as it is and at the same time be faced with pleas such as "I wish you wouldn't remind so many people that if the Xs get more, the Ys will lose something. Don't you care about the Xs?" Most sociologists reply that they must tell it as it is and clear the air, give the bad news with the good. And if we are going to understand upward and downward movement on the income scale at all fully, and the effects of different personality, intelligence, family, school, and economic factors on this movement, we need to leave the world of definitions and concepts for a while and ask a series of questions about what actually has been going on. The first place to understand mobility, and its relative absence for many, is in our historical past as a nation.

Social Mobility: From Covered Wagon to Corporate America

"Go West, Young Man" was a saying that began to have currency at the beginning of the 1800s, although there had been gradual expansion toward the open spaces for years before this time. The aim of the move was "getting ahead." The primary image was the covered wagon, the Conestoga, packed with a family's belongings and all their tools for farming. They were heading west for more land. In order to buy those wagons, they had to sell almost everything else. Recent calculations indicate that if we allow for inflation, they were worth then about the same as two Mercedes-Benzes today.

It was not the most successful who headed west, for they were happy where they were. But it was not the poor either. They had to stay where they were or wander from city to city in the East, for it took some real money to move. Rather, a new generation neither rich nor poor had caught the fever of upward mobility, of "bettering themselves," and hungered for the chance to make a new start in a new place.[23]

With each passing decade the industrial revolution began to take hold in the East, and immigrants arrived in waves to stock the jobs at the bottom of the social-class system. A social myth, often accepted by sociologists, began at this time. The myth went this way: In the years of the industrial revolution and then up to the start of the present century, things were wider open for personal advance-

ment than they are at present. If things are harder now, it is because
we have no frontier and industry has stopped growing. In those days,
well, anything was possible. This is an important issue—whether
things are significantly worse now than they have been in terms of
chances for advancement beyond the position of one's parents. If it
has almost always been hard to advance, then the promise of America
means something different than if the present is simply a tough
episode in an otherwise open social-advancement picture. Social historians using the research approaches of sociology began to get involved in this problem about a decade ago.

Let's begin with a few definitions, then consider a case history.
Social stratification is the sociologist's equivalent of the rock layers, or
strata of geology. A measure, or combination of measures, of social
status is created by the sociologists. One of the most common combi-
nations in use involves the following factors, or variables: income
level, years of schooling, occupational position, fanciness or simplic-
ity of home or residence area. Individuals can be scored on each of
these factors. A point score is made up by the sociologist. It is arbi-
trary in terms of how many points are given to each factor, but it is
applied equally to all the individuals scored. Then the total scores can
be used to place individuals in *social classes,* again with division decided by the researchers. One common classification is a five-class
division—upper class, upper middle, lower middle, upper lower, and
welfare. Another is a six-class division, seperating the upper class
into "old family" money and the newly rich. The main point of
scoring is to be able to compare individuals and groups of individuals,
such as families, ethnic groups, and racial groups, in terms of their
class standing. For example, you can ask questions such as "In our
scoring scheme, how many blacks are in the upper class, as compared
with whites?"

Social mobility is movement from class to class, up or down, by an
individual or group, using the classification system above. The movement may be from one generation to the next—"What class are you
in, and what was your father's?" Or it may be within a generation,
in an individual's life—"What class did you start out in, where were
you at mid-life, and where were you at retirement?" Our case study
will ask questions about stratification and mobility for American
society at the time of our industrial revolution. What did the stratification picture look like from 1830 to 1880? How easy or difficult was

social mobility within one's own lifetime, or from one generation to the next, in particular groups?

Stephan Thernstrom, a social historian interested in this problem, chose the small city of Newburyport, Massachusetts, on the Merrimac River where it meets the Atlantic Ocean and forms a natural harbor, as his location for a study of social mobility in the 1800s.[24] Newburyport (which other community sociologists have called "Yankee City") had a golden age of shipping in the early 1800s, when it was a clipper-ship port as big as Boston and Salem. Great colonial mansions were built on High Street, overlooking the harbor. But this boom time was succeeded by an era of economic depression. The ships went south as Boston's port grew, and the depression lasted until the industrial revolution crept downriver from Lowell and Lawrence. Factories then grew in Newburyport. As they grew, so did two kinds of labor. These were people from the surrounding farms—farm hands and poor farmers, plus their daughters—and Irish immigrants. By going through the old town records of births and deaths, marriage records and records of savings accounts in the local banks, Thernstrom was able to trace how fast people improved their "station in life" from one generation to the next. He was able to follow the first generation of factory workers and laborers from youth to retirement and follow as well the careers of their children. He assessed the degree to which the children of the first generation advanced beyond the social and economic status and occupational skills, of their fathers and mothers. Thus Thernstrom checked out both kinds of social mobility—*intragenerational* or your own mobility within your own life span, and *intergenerational*—how far you got with respect to your father or mother, or how far your children get with respect to you.

In general, Thernstrom found that the "wide-openness" of this booming industrial era was primarily a myth. Yankee (nonIrish) workers were able to put aside a little money and then possibly buy a small farm after twenty years of factory work. *Their* sons, the second-generation Yankee factory workers, tended to divide into two groups. Some wound up at about the same income and class level as their fathers. The others moved just one notch up, becoming foremen, for example. Or a nonfactory Yankee son whose father was a clerk would become a lawyer. But this was true only for the Yankees. The Irish, who had become a major group in town by the mid-1800s, showed hardly any mobility at all in an upward direction, and even some downward mobility in the slower periods. First-generation Irish retired with scarcely more than they started, and their children simply succeeded them in the ranks of unskilled labor and at the spinning jenny of the cotton mills.[25]

Thernstrom's findings are important because the picture they paint of one hundred years ago is so similar to the picture today, with blacks and other "third world" people substituted for the Irish. Historical studies of social mobility are increasingly beginning to paint a picture of our society as one with only small changes from one generation to the next. And even in the ranks of the upper middle class there are some downward falls; some sons and daughters go down the scale of income and social status. The idea that everyone or most everyone gets ahead is simply a myth. The past, like the present, shows a much crueler and more stagnant reality than the mythology of Horatio Alger of the rags-to-riches climb. Modern executives, for example, almost always come not from working-class backgrounds, but from the families of professionals and managers.[26] In general, the facts discoverable from much recent social inventory show a society with class lines a lot firmer than we like to think, and not much more open to social climbing up the income and class ladder than those of Western Europe, which have always been thought to be rigidly stratified in class terms. How, then, is the myth of an open society preserved in the face of a really near-closed society? The answer has been sought by a recent set of studies, which we take up next.

Factors Affecting Mobility and What Can Be Done About Them

Sociology and the other social sciences are only now getting to the point where they are beginning to understand the different factors that affect the future of individuals. A whole area of research is concerned with these issues. By way of introduction, at least the following factors affect social mobility: native ability, the interaction of ability and environment; the effects of school; the job-contact network; the number of job openings; job qualifications, real and unreal; employer prejudice; and the overall class structure of the society, especially the political influence of the corporation over the economy. Each is a field of research that we can only touch on here, and each is in process of development.

Native ability, or genetic endowment, has been found by recent studies to have minimal effect on school achievement, and achievement in school is in turn not very closely associated with performance on the job. One kind of situation, though, does give a head start to some children. The bright child born to intellectual and intelligent college educated, upper-middle-class parents will often interact at home. The parents will often teach their children to read before school begins, giving them a head start and home support. These small differences in native ability of the children get exaggerated and magnified at school. A vicious cycle can develop. Christopher Jencks and his colleagues observe:

> Genetic influences of this sort are likely to exert their influence very early, and they are likely to become more important as children get older. There seems, for example, to be an association between the amount a mother talks to her child and the child's subsequent verbal skills. If talking to the child is interesting and pleasant, most mothers will talk more than if the child is inarticulate . . . This cycle is likely to be repeated at school. The child who starts off with a small genetic advantage may learn quickly, receive encouragement, and learn more. The child who starts off with a small genetic disadvantage may learn more slowly, be discouraged by the teacher, and stop trying to learn at all. Small genetic differences may therefore end up producing big environmental differences and hence big differences in test scores.[27]

But note that scores on tests and grades, no matter how really slightly related to measuring native ability they might be, count as the main determiner of placement in the tracking system of most American junior high schools.

The Jencks group found that a lot of school factors were not very important in final achievement—for instance, the size of the class and the number of homework assignments. But they found that the family background and the type of community in which the school was set (poverty area versus fancy suburb) were very important. What the research shows, all in all, however, is that we can pick apart a complicated reality, piece by piece, and pretend that the factors such as school, home, and education of parents, work independently to produce effects, when they don't.

The transition from school to work is another example of how different parts of reality interrelate. Numerous studies have found that the kind of schooling one gets and the kind of job contacts one makes are importantly related. Mark Granovetter wrote a book with the simple title *Getting a Job.* In it he reports that a large proportion of the jobs found by people he studied were originally heard of through close friends, relatives, or people close to friends or relatives. As this suggests, the social circle of parents can lead to jobs for son and daughter.[28] For example, an upper-middle-class doctor's son is bankrolled through four years of an Ivy league college and three years at Harvard Law School. He then chooses to go back to his home town. There he uses both the prestige of this law degree and his father's golfing partner—the head of the main law firm in town—as two factors in getting a good start on a profitable law career, in a high-paying firm serving the large corporations of the area. Contrast this story with that of a truck-driver's son who takes two years at the local community college, does well, and transfers to the state university. He runs out of cash after college and gets a job, any job, and goes evenings to a law school "factory," gets a degree and sets up a storefront office in a working class neighborhood. He chases ambulances, does divorce work for poor clients, and just makes a living. Both young men have career patterns that abstractly read "college to law school to practice of law." One earns six times the salary of the other. They are in two separate worlds.[29]

What of the actual number of job openings? Much is made of the gap between the number of jobs available and the numbers of people looking for work, especially in this time of high general unemployment. There are a lot of school-dropout teenagers and unemployed laborers. But there are still a number of openings in communities all over the land for experienced computer programmers, legal secretaries who can spell accurately and have a college-level vocabulary, electronics technicians with five years of experience, and so on. The money needed to train or retrain a high proportion of our unskilled and underskilled people is not voted in Congress. This extra money for training is often opposed by both regular taxpayers and by corporations, because they will have to pay the bill for the training out of increased taxes. What may be developing, therefore, is a two-level job market with a lower level for the unskilled and a lot of women and an upper level primary for men with skilled training and college and a job-experience record.[30] How to get people into the top-level job market is a focus for much research and action by women and minorites at present. False barriers to jobs—requiring tests and credentials that don't really apply—are also under investigation and governmental review at present. Social scientists, including sociologists, often were the first to ring the alarm bell about the groups left out and the unfair barriers to hiring them as well. In general, a job opening is a funny thing. We must ask, open to whom? and Why only to them?

And then there is prejudice, plenty of it—sexism, racism, ageism, preference for "Americans" over those who speak with an accent. Recent laws passed by Congress have begun to deal with the problem, which involves both refusal to hire on grounds of race, sex, and so forth, and refusal to promote when promotion is warranted, on the basis of comparison with others in the same workplace. But HEW and the courts have been dragging their feet for many years now. Decisions in one jurisdiction conflict with those in another, and a more conservative Supreme Court is no longer in the forefront of change. It has taken much political struggle by those affected by the prejudice to get even minimal gains. We will pay special attention to the problems of women and work, but the entire area of discrimination and prejudice has been one of major importance to sociologists.

Finally, another general interpretation of this blocked opportunity situation is presented by the modern Marxian theoretical point of view. This approach begins with the observation that most work places are owned by others and the jobs, salaries, and opportunities of the workers are manipualted by these others in the interests of their short-run or long-run profit. It also makes the observation that the word "class" is used often as I introduced it above, to stand for scores on social stratification scoring scales. But the word has a more specific and different meaning in Marxian theory. There it refers to a group of people classified according to where they are with respect to the production of goods and services. Are they owners of the factories or other workplaces? If so they belong to the owning class, large capitalists and small storekeepers are two subdivisions of this class. Or are they employees, those who do *not* own the place in which they work? If so, they belong to the Marxian "working class." The economic interests and political action of classes are the main point here, rather than comparisons of status and mobility, the main purpose and use of standard social-class rating scales.

From this other theoretical viewpoint, a high rate of unemployment is characteristic of any modern capitalist society because *the un.mployment works against those employed,* preventing them from demanding higher wages. "You are lucky to have a job at all," states the employer during hard times, "so if you want too much I will fire you, and if you strike I'll replace you with someone out of work." In addition, the racial and ethnic divisions of working people against one another (black against white, factory workers against craftsmen, Spanish-speaking against English-speaking) act against their all getting together to push for the interests of all as a whole group. Employers sometimes exploit this philosophy of "me first and the hell with you." It prevents these people from combining and being able to fight as a larger and thus stronger group to improve their position as a whole class, in the Marxian sense. At the same time, these individuals accept the society's present definition of their situation and their chances and almost always blame *themselves* for their failure, when in reality as the Marxian viewpoint sees it, an entire economy is stacked against them.

On Women's Work

Louise Howe recently joined working women and worked along with them at a set of jobs—beautician, salesclerk in a department store, waitress, office worker. She worked for pay as a regular worker for about three months, got to know the people on the job, and then turned interviewer, combining her observations with direct interviews in depth.[31] She found much drudgery in these typical women's occupations, extremely low pay, hostility and scorn from male bosses, and disinterest on the part of unions. The sales job, in the dress department of the department store, was typical. The pay was low and the work exhausting, and no salesperson was allowed to sit down. In addition, she began to notice the store was hiring part-time women workers at minimum wages. The early shift was women with children in school, the afternoon-to-evening shift students and single women. All made slightly more than one gets on welfare. Ms. Howe asked Andrea, the "personnel lady," whether this was because the company made money by paying the cheaper wages to part-timers. Andrea replied:

> Yes, that's certainly one of the factors. You can cover yourself during these rush hours and have less people when its quieter. Also there can be some savings on fringe benefits a company has to pay. If you work here

a month you have to join the union, and that means, if you're full time you're immediately eligible for health insurance. But if you're part-time you have to wait six months, by which time many of our part-timers are gone. Also we only have to provide health insurance if you're not covered elsewhere.[32]

The most important dimension of women's work, one that has been central in the investigations of sociologists and economists, has been such economic exploitation of most working women. A second dimension that sociologists have covered in depth has been the sexism of the wider society as it is found in the world of work. This forces women into segregated, stereotyped, dead-end occupations and also blocks their career advancement to higher-paying and more interesting jobs.

A sociologist approaching a problem such as this first tries to get an accurate idea of what the problem really is. For example, if women are paid less than men, what does that mean? If women are routinely prevented from entering the higher-paying jobs as easily as men do and if schools routinely track them into office-clerical training or some such before they look for work, then their average wage will be less than men's because the jobs they will get are routinely low-paying. This is an *opportunity* problem, with a school-bias problem making it more severe. If women do the exact same work as a man and are paid less for it, that's an *equality* problem. In fact, the statistics gathered over the years by sociologists, economists, and government bureaus such as the U.S. Department of Labor find both kinds of discrimination affecting women with the situation worse now than ten years ago. Matched against men, in 1965, women as a group made $2500 less than a man's salary, as of 1973 they made $5000 less.[33]

The occupations that are classically defined as women's work are almost always lower-paying than men's jobs because they are defined that way. When secretaries and typists were male in the early years of this century, they were paid as junior staff members or white-collar clerks with a chance for promotion. They were in a kind of "management trainee" role. When these occupations became "feminized," the salaries were lowered and the chances for advancement disappeared. Edward Gross did a historical and statistical review of the degree of sex segregation of occupations—the extent to which they were marked out as "male" or "female" work. He found that the degree of sex segregation of jobs had not changed markedly from 1900 to the mid-1960s.[34] If more women were entering the labor force at this time instead of staying home, it was into "female" jobs —store clerk, waitress, beautician. In addition, when women have successfully moved into a new occupation as a group, "feminizing" it, wages have often been deliberately lowered by employers. This is similar to banks and real estate firms' lowering property values and refusing to guarantee mortgages when nonwhites move into a neighborhood. A parallel exists between this kind of racism and sexism in job wages and occupational opportunity. Gross sums it up this way:

> The movement of women into the labor market has not meant the disappearance of sexual typing in occupation. Rather, the great expansion in female employment has been accomplished through the expansion of occupations that were already female, through the emergence of wholly new occupations (such as that of key punch operator) which were defined as female from the start, and through females taking over previously male occupations. This last may be compared to the process of racial invasion in American cities. From the group's point of view, such invasion provides new opportunities, but still in a segregated context.[35]

Another reason why women's wages are as low as they are is the disinterest of the majority of America's labor unions in women and their working conditions and wages. Observing this and also seeing that it is harder to unionize part-time workers than full-time ones, many businessmen prefer the female part-timers to full-timers. Seeing often both disinterest and open sexism on the part of many union organizers and officers, women reject the unions. The percentage of women in unions has been going down at even a faster rate than the percentage of all workers in unions (which has also been going down for a variety of reasons). In organizations where there is both union and nonunion work, for example different departments in a big store, the male occupations are far more likely to be unionized than the female. One ray of hope here lies in the "overtrained woman" phenomenon—the increasing numbers of women college graduates becoming secretaries and waitresses. With more education and higher expectations, they are both more likely to get angry at their treatment and more willing to organize politically against these conditions. Thus the role of unions in the area of women's work may soon be entering a new phase, one that could revitalize the union movement itself as well as advance the interests of women. But there is a long way to go.[36]

What is "career advancement" for women today? Unfortunately, the sociological and the activist books and speeches are so concentrated on this issue that a lot of women are ignored in the process. For example, in her groundbreaking book *The Feminine Mystique* Betty Friedan basically was urging college-educated women to get out of the house and find rewarding, high-level jobs.[37] For more than a century many working-class women had to get out and work in industry in order to gain enough money to keep the family alive. For many of these women, "advancement" always meant not having to work at such jobs. On the other hand, the barriers to the advancement of women in the professions and in the higher ranks of the business world are clear. A woman's sex and any family ties she may have are used to disqualify her, but not a man who has precisely the same kind of ties. At a major industrial corporation in which she carried out a field participant-observation study, Rosabeth Kanter found this:

> Two single women, one of them forty, in quite different functions, were told by their managers that they could not be given important jobs because they were likely to get married and leave . . . On the other hand, they were told also in other circumstances that married women cannot be given important jobs because of their family responsibilities: their children, if they are working mothers; their unborn children and the danger they will leave with pregnancy, if currently childless.[38]

These arguments have been used for generations as excuses for keeping women "in their place." Only pressure form the women's movement has led to notable increases in enrollment of women in medical school. The movement successfully pushed for increases twice—in its original incarnation in the middle to late 1800s and again in the mid-1970s.[39] The reasoning about women having "ties" that disqualify them for advancement has been used in one place that is embarrassing for me to report. It has been used by male chairmen in predominantly male sociology departments in universities. The group Sociologists for Women in Society, or SWS, was formed ten years ago by female sociologists to eliminate sexism from the lecture platform in sociology courses and from the department's workings as well. An occasional male supporter joined, too. The Old-Boy network of academia has been a barrier to women. Especially in graduate schools at elite universities male friends have gotten each other and each others' proteges jobs in their schools without even announcing the availability of the jobs. Fighting fire with fire, SWS set up an Old-Girl network. Much as I am in sympathy with the problem, as I understand things this will not solve the problem, but simply add another part to it. What about those, male or female, who did not go to grad school at an elite university or don't have a powerful sponsor but just happen to be good teachers? Still, the fight of SWS and similar groups elsewhere in academia has been an important and necessary one, leading to valuable and badly needed courses on sex roles, as well as more understanding of the social and economic problems of women. The fight goes on, within as well as outside of academia.[40] As I have said about them before, sociologists are not unanimous in their opinion on any social issue. Some sociologists, such as Nathan Glazer, are in the forefront of action against requiring more equality in hiring and promotion in universities.[41] Their argument is that boat rocking by government will cause more backlash than it is worth. I personally think their argument is a weak one simply justifying inaction. There are legal issues here which are complex and very real, but they are not being advanced by this group of sociologists. This pro-and-con fight going on between progressives and conservatives in sociology might be an intriguing one for you to read up on and decide for yourself where you stand.

In general, sociology serves as a mirror, a reflector, and an inciter to questions. I have just spent a lot of time on one question—the issue of opportunity for women—to show how sociology approaches it. Sociology is not usually a beautifier of the society in which it is allowed to freely function. Also, it is not usually in the vanguard of new attitudes. But it isn't too far behind. For example, sociologists as a total group have not taken the lead in areas such as sex discrimination and racial discrimination in employment, but some sociological voices have been heard to speak out frequently from the sidelines, and the majority of the profession is frequently among the first to take up the torch in support of the pioneers.

The next step is often new courses in sociology departments to deal with the issue—"Women and Work," "The Sexual Role Revolution," and "The Changing American Family." These new courses and the new points of view they present have been contributing to the education of a whole new generation of college students. They inform them that the old social rules and customs are not written in stone. They say these rules and customs should be inspected and a *choice* made to continue accepting them or to replace them with other ways of acting.

Sociological questions about work address themselves also to another great area—the structure and function of the work setting itself. How is it as a place to be? What is the significance of the way it is arranged? This area of research can help with your choice of a place to work yourself and add to your understanding of what happens when you arrive there. We turn to it next.

The Workplace: Home or Iron Cage?

Before the industrial revolution and even in the first few decades after it was under way, most Americans worked in small settings. They worked in their homes or small shops, in stores, on farms nearby. A walk down the main streets of old colonial Williamsburg, Virginia, which reproduces this situation, will reveal a small number of people at work in each small shop. With the onset of modern industry came the modern bureaucratic way of organizing work, with large numbers of people in one place, under one boss or owner. Max Weber, the first great sociological student of bureaucracy, defined the "ideal," or perfectly functioning, bureaucracy as an organization with a clear chain of command from the top down. He said it had an organization chart with carefully described job slots and had occupants in each slot who did exactly what they were paid to do following the rules of the organization and their job description to the letter. The customers of such an ideal bureaucracy would all be treated exactly alike, according to the rules of "customer treatment"; no favorites would be played. Communication would flow without interruption from the top down and the bottom up, and would not be distorted in either direction.[42]

This model of people organized to act as a smoothly running, well-oiled machine was seldom found in reality, and Weber admitted as much. After all, this was the perfect or "ideal" image of a bureaucracy, used to compare real ones against. But Weber also noted that by 1900 more and more work settings—and school settings—were becoming organized in this manner. The onset of modern capitalism, especially its interest in making human work arrangements more efficient and workplaces more productive to increase profits of the owners of the place, seemed to push more and more people into this form of social organization. In addition some came voluntarily, leaving lives of rural poverty for hopes of gain in the new factories. Weber worried about this bureaucratizing of the world. He feared its ultimate consequences, especially the implications for human freedom in such places, and he feared a society organized this way, from the top to the bottom.[43] He called such a future society "the iron cage."

A second and a third generation of sociologists have gone over this ground since Weber wrote. The studies that have been done give grounds for both optimism and pessimism. Unlike Weber, the later sociologists have concentrated on the real instead of comparing the real with a single ideal. They have focused more closely on the social process in bureaucratically organized workplaces. They have in general contrasted this social reality, found through participant observation in most cases, with the formal organization chart found in the place—the way it was versus the way the people in the organization told the researcher that the organization was supposed to look on the chart. They have contrasted the official image of the organization presented to outsiders with its reality. And they have found what I would call grounds for hope and optimism, in people's ability to be innovative and to resist a regimented life at work. But they have also found the trend toward more and more thorough bureaucracy that Weber described, and a large proportion of people either actively pushing to further bureaucratize the work setting or simply passively sitting back and letting the chips fall where they may. A few of these studies can help to illustrate the ways that sociologists have studied the issue of the organization of work in modern society.

The Organization Observed

Three studies, among many excellent ones, will be singled out here. They are the mid-fifties classic which named an important social phenomenon, William H. Whyte's *Organization Man*;[44] Michel Crozier's participant-observation study in two French organizations in the early sixties, which he named *The Bureaucratic Phenomenon;*[45] and Rosabeth Kanter's recent study of men and women in a giant business organization in the mid-seventies, *Men and Women of the Corporation*.[46] These three share a set of themes, but each builds on the previous decade of work in this area. A brief review can help convey a sense of what sociologists are up to when they study large, complex bureaucratic organizations.

Whyte was concerned with the self in the organization, the pressures toward conformity and "going along," and ways in which the large corporation tended to own and influence far more of the executive's life than just the hours at work. For example, Whyte talked with the wives of rising young executives (this was the fifties and female excutives were almost nonexistent). He found that informal social life was organized by neighborhood, especially in "company towns" where the firm he was studying was the largest employer. A promotion in the organization led, they felt, to pressure on them to move. They also felt they were expected to break off close friendships with those who did not get promoted and stayed behind in the old, less fancy neighborhood.[47] But Whyte's most important findings, in chapter after chapter, stressed the passivity and helplessness felt by the majority of the workers, especially the executives who were his main focus for research. They felt the corporation controlled their lives. Tested, filed, catalogued, and inspected by personality tests and interviews for conformity, they feared to stand out. They feared especially being put in a position where they had to oppose the organization and speak for themselves.[48]

A minority of the executives were old-fashioned fighters, risk-takers who still could claw their way to the top or lose and get fired. But the majority "went along," even when the organization moved them and their families from place to place as often as once a year. Movement was usually interpreted as exposure to new branches of the corporation, preparing the executive for a big move up. But the fear nagged that the company was just moving them around to suit *its* convenience rather than because of any real interest in promotion. The organization's right to totally determine careers was not questioned by these men. One said:

> I hope the company isn't playing checkers with me. I feel a lack. I don't know what I'm being groomed for. I don't know what contacts to keep alive. A sales manager knows he should keep his customer contacts, but in the broad management philosophy you can't do this. You have to guess. I felt I had trained for twenty years for a tremendous job that had plenty of challenge, and I was in it for only nine months. Somehow, I feel this move is out of my pattern—whatever that is. I'd hate to lose all that's behind me because somebody is playing checkers with me.[49]

In the 1960s, as antiestablishment and antiauthority sentiment grew, rigid organizational arrangements and demands for conformity were increasingly resisted. For example, the Free Speech Movement in Berkeley, California, originally was a protest by students against the impersonal bureaucracy of the University of California. The group took its slogan from student enrollment cards—"Do Not Fold, Spindle, or Mutilate [Us]." For many, this spirit soon left its original target and was directed against the war in Vietnam. But some of the spirit remained directed at the original target—Max Weber's iron cage. In France, the workers were becoming increasingly restive, and by the late sixties were close to a union with the Left that in 1968 led to a near-revolutionary situation.[50] Michel Crozier, a sociologist, had studied French bureaucratic organizations at the start of this period. He began to notice ways that those at a low level in organizations have of increasing their freedom of action, of fighting against the encroachments of the iron cage, even if production, or whatever the place is supposed to be engaged in, is slowed considerably by these actions. They acted to *limit* the demands of management to a tolerable level. Evidence from France (and this country) indicates the phenomena have been around a long time, but may simply have been a little more observable during this decade, especially with the protest movements as active as they were and giving heart to workers' willingness to *express* discontent.

Crozier found that most lower-level workers were able to frustrate the effectiveness of the chain of command by the simple act of refusing to hand accurate information on their activity up the line and by using their needed skills as potential blackmail. Cooperation of lower-level workers is essential to the bosses of such a place, he found, and the bosses' power to handle these workers is never complete. In the French government bureaucracy, one of his settings, Crozier found that lower-level workers perceived resistance by themselves as a strategy for increasing their breathing room. If the organization's effectiveness was blocked as a consequence, the workers were quite willing to sacrifice it.[51] Erving Goffman, in a study of mental hospitals, found something quite similar. "Colonizing" the round-the-clock institution, such as a prison, mental hospital, or wealthy boarding school, meant personalizing the impersonal walls and corners and sabotaging the ability of the organization to watch what was going on.[52] The human spirit, apparently, resists over-bureaucratization.

But not completely. In the seventies Rosabeth Kanter visited precisely the same kind of organization Whyte studied in the fifties. Not much was different. For one thing, she found that the tight job market of the seventies had handed power back to the employer, that had begun to rise on the worker side during the preceding period of higher employment and activist protest. I think this is the return of a cycle. Just as the owners of restaurants sometimes take a "shut up or get fired" attitude toward a waitress who wants a rest period, so many organizations are returning to pre-sixties attitudes toward requirements of conformity and obedience by employees, who know that their only alternative might be welfare.

Kanter noted some minor differences, such as pressure from government to give women some positions in management. She found tokenism in evidence all over the corporation—not the same as significant progress for the majority. Career insecurities for both men and women, especially organizational careers as a race with a vast mass of losers and only a few driven, work-monopolized winners, seem not to have changed at all, in the last twenty years.[53]

Sociologists have studied careers and life styles that are alternatives to the career in the organization. Kanter herself, for example, has studied rural communes, which combine group living with group self-sufficient activity. This turns out to be a lot of work, more than many had bargained for, but for those who stay, it is a human and personal kind of work and not, whatever else, bureaucratic.[54] Other sociologists have studied the growth of craft occupations and stores. They indicate that there is a growing interest in un-bureaucratic ways of organizing work.

Other studies deal with attempts to humanize standard organizations. They show that minor innovations are possible. But the attempts are limited in almost every case by the profit motives of management—too much flexibility has been found to be extremely expensive. In addition, much work is broken down into little units that can be done by anyone, allowing employers to pay low wages to the relatively unskilled people who are hired to do them. As long as workers do not have a major say in their working conditions, which they do not because of their lack of both control and ownership of most American workplaces now, major limits are created for changes. This implies, of course, a direction that workers might go in the future, in terms of political action.

Sociology, Work, and You

For the independently wealthy, work can always be chosen for what it provides in the way of fulfillment, challenge, or just plain fun. For the rest of us, work is a necessity. Studying the sociology of work experience, opportunity for jobs, and the work setting is not usually a good way to find a specific job. But sociological perspectives on work and careers and their rewards and pitfalls can have value for you as you approach the world of work.

First, everyone has at the back of their minds a picture of a lifelong career or at least a way of making a living for themselves. But along the way a lot of stereotypes about work have been presented. At home, in elementary school, in junior high, in part-time jobs in the summer, a lot of information has been presented to many people. Much of it actually is false and distorted. Sociological study in the area of occupations and work organizations can help you sort the stereotypes from reality. This is particularly true for the times you are told that something "isn't possible" and "why it isn't." Sociological study can give you understanding of the broad social forces that operate to channel people into unfulfilling and unrewarding work. This understanding may help you avoid some pitfalls and dead ends that aren't apparent at first glance.

Second, though much has been said here about opportunity and its absence, several things should not be taken personally. No responsible sociologist, including myself, would suggest that so many cards are stacked against you that you ought not to try your best, using what training and skills you can muster, to succeed in the present society if that is really your aim in life. Sociology does not provide an excuse for passivity; if anything, studies by researchers—Jencks, for instance—show that personal characteristics, including the willingness to work hard, can make some difference in later career and income.

But sociology doesn't promise you that the world out there is a rose garden either. And if the news is bad, sociologists will usually not hide the fact. The critical left within sociology and the establishment center agree about the rather low amount of upward mobility from generation to generation—it does exist, of course. Beyond this, they disagree about *why* there isn't much upward mobility and what if anything should be done about that. This debate within the field is a mirror of an argument that is heating up right now in the whole society. Some people, especially those doing very well at the present game with the present rules (is this you and your parents?), want the social game and the rules left alone. Others, especially those from poor and working class homes, many women, non-whites, homosexuals, and the people whose first language is not English, think that the game is rigged, with rules applied by a judge who has been bribed. Since sociologists disagree here, it can be a challenge for you to find out the details on this debate. Then you can decide where you stand on the basis of your own thinking and not on what you were told. In the process you'll learn more about the factors affecting your opportunity and that of others. Again, some people have grown up in homes where all those on welfare were described as lazy cheaters and such, until their father or mother loses a job and a painful reappraisal begins. For some, these very issues cause discomfort just to think about. But what is a liberal education, anyway, but growth and the pain that sometimes goes with it? The big picture—the economic and political forces in the wider society—all have their consequences for individual lives, including yours. Whether you decide to go with the existing system or work to change it, courses in the sociology of education, race relations, in social problems, and other related areas, will help in developing your own stand.

Third, what about a job or career? If you are undecided at this point, study in the sociology of work, occupations, and mobility may help you separate the myth from the reality, especially in areas of work you presently have some interest in. It can help you weigh the opportunities and the challenges against the problems. Both quantitative, large scale survey studies and the more intimate field participant-observation studies will help to develop a feel for kinds of work, and a set of further questions to ask. Organizations, especially large and impersonal ones, are only one kind of place to work. Can some of them be humanized? Other kinds of work arrangments are developing. There is a low-visibility social movement by people who want to develop their own jobs, and also a return to the crafts. Sociological study in this broad area should do more than provide information, however. It should provide a set of general ideas that you can use as handles on the complex realities of work. In the years to come, these should help you understand the work that *others* are doing, as well as your own.

Finally, a sociological perspective on work will constantly remind you that no work or career exists in a vacuum. In the prevailing work world, we tend to have each working person making his or her own lonely way, much as an explorer hacks through an uncharted jungle. Is the system responsive to such lonely individuals, or does it eat them up, picking them off one by one, like the proverbial man-eating tiger? Do you think people would do better to work together in larger groups and push for real change, as the fifteen drawbridge operators did in New York City? What do our political parties, our unions, or any action groups, have to say about this basic issue? Or are they silent? Do the corporations control the economy to the extent that they can frustrate opportunity and keep unemployment up without difficulty to themselves? I can't even begin to answer these questions here, just raise them. (We will return to them in Chapter 5, *Acting Politically.*) But considering what you might do about the overall setup within which you look for work, and build a work life, involves looking at what the sociologists are arguing about here.

For Further Reading

Emile Durkheim. *The Division of Labor in Society.* Glencoe, Illinois: Free Press, 1947.
  This work presents contrast between societies governed by custom and a non-Western technology, where most people do the same work, and our modern world, with its specializing of work. Deals also with the consequences of our kind of division of work.
Everett Hughes. *Men and Their Work.* New York: Free Press, 1958.
  Treats the human side of work, the play of forces between individuals and their work roles. A series of essays that has become a modern classic and has inspired many field studies of occupations and professions at work.
Marcia Millman. *The Unkindest Cut.* New York: Morrow, 1977.
  Millman contrasts the public face of the medical profession, especially surgeons, to a private world of secrets and mutual protection against outside observation and review of doctor's work. Report of a field study in three hospitals.
Christopher Jencks, Marshall Smith, Henry Acland, Mary Jo Bane, David Cohen, Herbert Gintis, Berbara Heyns, and Stephan Michelson. *Inequality: A Reassessment of the Effect of Family and Schooling in America.* New York: Harper & Row, 1973.
  Using national survey and testing data, as well as income data, these

researchers assessed how family, schooling, and other factors help reproduce social-class position from generation to generation.

Stephan Thernstrom. *Proverty and Progress: Social Mobility in a Nineteenth Century City.* Cambridge, Mass.: Harvard University Press, 1964.

Getting ahead in the mid-1800s, in Newburyport, Massachusetts, depended a lot on whether you were Irish or not, but even for Yankees the opportunities were rather limited. This well-written and innovative social history demolishes the myth of "wide-open" America.

Mark Granovetter. *Getting a Job: A Study of Contacts and Careers.* Cambridge: Harvard University Press 1974.

How do people find jobs? Before Granovetter, no one did good research on just how newspaper ads, personal and family contacts, and employment offices were really used and by whom, and whether they paid off or not. Contacts are very important, Granovetter found, which does not paint a pretty picture for a poor person looking for a job.

Richard Sennett and Jonathan Cobb. *Hidden Injuries of Class.* New York: Random House, 1973.

What it's like to be a loser, by losers. Sennett and Cobb interview ordinary working people who have not been overly successful, and inspect ways that society trains people to blame all their lost opportunity, or their lack of it in the first place, on themselves. Beautifully written.

Louise Kapp Howe. *Pink Collar Workers.* New York: Morrow, 1977.

Ms. Howe takes you with her right into the department store, the beauty parlor, and other places where women work. Then she discusses the impact of our present occupational system on women, with figures. An important and very readable book.

Rosabeth Moss Kanter. *Men and Women of the Corporation.* New York: Basic Books, 1977.

In a sense, Whyte's *Organization Man,* of the fifties redone for the seventies, again by way of participant observation, Kanter pays as much attention to the fate of women in the corporation as the fate of men. The big corporation grinds on almost as if the sixties hadn't happened. Important and scholarly.

HEW. *Work in America: Report to the Secretary of HEW from the Secretary's Commission on Work in America.* Cambridge, Mass.: M.I.T. Press, 1973.

This government report is quite useful as a list of problems and issues. Well written, not "bureaucratic."

Harry Braverman. *Labor and Monopoly Capital.* New York: Monthly Review Press, 1975.

A clearly written, nonjargony critique of the problems presented by the preceding report. The book has a Marxian theoretical framework that includes the profit motive of employers and discusses "degradation of work"—chopping it into little pieces—as a characteristic of capitalism in large factories. Important book.

Chapter

FOUR

Joining A Community

Carl Sandburg, one of our great American poets, came to Chicago at a time of roaring expansion, during the first decades of this century. He sang this song in awe and wonder:

> *Chicago*
> Hog Butcher for the World
> Tool maker, Stacker of Wheat
> Player with Railroads and the Nation's Freight Handler
> Stormy, husky, brawling,
> City of the Big Shoulders[1]

The city was marked by the colors and sounds of its commerce:

> Mention proud things, catalogue them.
> The jack-knife bridge opening, the ore boats,
>   the wheat passing through.
> Three overland trains arriving at the same hour,
>   one from Memphis and the cotton belt,
>   one from Omaha and the corn belt,
>   one from Duluth, the lumberjack and the iron range.
> Mention a carload of shorthorns taken off the valleys of
>   Wyoming last
>   week, arriving yesterday, knocked in the head, stripped,
>   quartered,

tion the daily melodrama of this hum-
drum, rhythm of
heads, hides, heels, hoofs hung up.[2]

For this poet each city was unique, and yet Chicago was "the city,"
the symbol. And the city, in the last analysis, was its people:

Every day the people sleep and the city dies;
every day the people shake loose, awake, and
build the city again.[3]

And it was Chicago, Sandburg's Chicago, that saw the beginning
of American community sociology and was in some ways the cause
of it.[4] This brings up a basic question. We know why poets are
interested, but why do sociologists study communities? Two reasons
come to mind immediately and will be the focus for this chaper. First,
the sense of community—the way that the people make the city, a
feeling of place and of belonging to others and to a neighborhood—
is a basic element of an integrated social life. In times of crisis its
absence has dire consequences because of absence of social support;
the presence of a sense of community adds enjoyment to everyday
life. Second, *the fact of community*—the pattern of social relationships
across the map including the power structure that ties the map together—is a basic building block of most societies. The community
is about the largest social unit we can encompass with our experience
instead of as a headline in the newspaper or some other abstraction.
Communities are the key bridge between the family and the nation,
a focus for most of the crises of the present era.

The questions the first generation of American urban sociologists
at Chicago asked about communities are still valuable, still worth
asking. This is especially true of the ones asked by Robert Park, one
of American sociology's founders, so we will take up his questions
as our first step in looking at communities sociologically. Then it will
be useful to look at the ways in which one sociologist found out
about a community, how he went about asking questions and doing
community field research. Next, it will help to look at the phenomenon of community as a complex puzzle, changing its parts in different
times and places. Has a community changed? How did it get to be

the community it now is, and where is it going in the future? Then there is the issue of *power* and the community power structure that ties these areas together, or tears them apart. Who wins, and loses in the community battles, and why? What are the implications of some trends here? Finally, what does all this have to do with your own experience? I asked just such a set of questions about my own small town, and got into a community fight for the preservation of Pleasant Valley—my neighborhood. From these different viewpoints, at the conclusion of the chapter I will speak about your applying the sociological approach to a community of your own, in order to really discover where you live and who you are living with.

Chicago: The Birth of Community Sociology

When Maynard Hutchins convinced John D. Rockefeller to pay for a new university to crown the expansion of Chicago and give it a cultural center the equal of its commerce, a problem remained— faculty. How could people of national and international reputation be lured out into this big, brawling, raw midwestern city from their genteel Eastern ivory towers and cultured communities? Some wouldn't come for any reason. But for others, as Rockefeller must have noted, the answer was money—lots of it, double the salary their colleges were paying them elsewhere in some cases. But the newness of the University of Chicago had a special attraction for intellectuals whose discipline was new, whose field was just getting started. So when Albion Small, one of America's first sociologists, was asked if he was interested in joining the new university, he said yes—on one condition. This was that the university set up a sociology department. "A what?" was the first response. But Small, the president of Oberlin College in Ohio, convinced the university builders that sociology was the wave of the future. They then agreed to provide him with his department, and they began to like the idea, for Chicago was to be the city of the future. Thus it was that the Middle West nurtured American sociology in its early days (the Columbia University department got under way soon after this time). And Chicago, a natural sociology laboratory, and Robert Park, one of Small's first stars, revolutionized American sociology. They turned it from an armchair discipline into a field-study operation.[5]

Park, a newpaper reporter before he became a sociologist, kept his reporter's keen curiosity, and when he became a professor at Chicago, he set an agenda for research on the city. In a long and influential article in the *American Journal of Sociology* in 1915, he laid out a program of research which to this day is still being followed in that some of its basic questions are still being asked by community sociologists.[6] To begin with, he urged his first students, who were soon to go out and invent community research, to define the community as a social system. He described a community social system as an arragement of people who either shared or did not share common assumptions about morality, business, the law, politics, and the future of the area. The system was bounded by natural and man-made geographical features. Describe the community as it is, Park urged, not as you might like it to be.

Park asked three kinds of questions in his key article: questions about the human and social meaning of neighborhoods to people, about the division of the city into "natural areas," and about the political forces that worked to preserve a city or change it. Underlying all his specific questions were two general ones about the contrast between the city and the country. How does the city affect the "moral order" and the relationships that make for a stable society? How was the order backed in turn by the social rules and values that people bring with them to the city and use as a guide to life while there? Does living in a city have a major impact on social life over and above the change that occurs in relationships and customs elsewhere? He and the other sociologists at Chicago had another, more personal reason for asking. Many were sons of preachers and farmers, and almost all were country boys, as shaken by Chicago in their way as Sandburg was in his.

About neighborhoods, Park observed that living near to people and neighborly contact constituted "the basis for the simplest and most elementary form of association . . . in the organization of city life." He further observed that "it is important to know what are the forces which tend to break up the tensions, interests, and sentiments which give neighborhoods their individual character."[7] In general, he viewed neighborhoods, especially ethnic neighborhoods, as organizations that protected their people against the disorder and impersonality of the city as a whole.[8] They were defensive in function, allowing newcomers to feel at home in a new land, and would be deserted by the next generation, as they moved to more expensive housing elsewhere.

Park's second set of questions were historical in nature. They had to do with the growth and development of what he called "natural areas" of the city—in the case of Chicago the ghettos, high-rent districts, business districts, stockyards, and railroad areas. How did they develop? What immigrant groups arrived to change these areas from one language or color to the next? Where did the old population move when it was replaced in an area by a new wave of migrants? And in general—the central theme of all his work—how did the industrialization and modernization of society, seen at its peak in the cities, affect all aspects of the quality of life? To Park, the city was a living puzzle, and the pieces were to be viewed independently and in their relationship to one another. He worried about breakdown of the social order, about social disorganization and impersonality.[9]

In this vein, the disorganization or breakdown of older village-wide social systems when they were transplanted the context of the cities led into Park to a sociological hypothesis about the origins of crime. He deliberately challenged those who said that Italian, Polish, and black people were genetically prone to crime. In general, he said, "It is probably the breaking down of local attachments and the weakening of the restraints and inhibitions of the primary group, under the influence of the urban environment, which are largely responsible for the increase of vice and crime in great cities." By "primary group" he meant the individual's closest social circle—family and close friends. Urban sociology of crime and delinquency and the whole field of the sociology of deviance began with thoughts such as these.[10]

Park was not slinging mud at immigrants and poor people. He was proposing a set of urban sociological research projects that would get at the differences in values and customs, including attitudes toward the law, between the dominant society and the neighborhood community.

Park's questions can be asked somewhere else besides a large city, but he offered Chicago as a natural laboratory for sociology student researchers. It was a place where social phenomena were perhaps more intense, more frequent, more findable.

As a reporter Park had been a muckraker—a specialist in corruption. Thus he was a student of city politics—the politics of Chicago's wards and political bosses in particular. He was interested in the power structure of cities. He would have been very much at home studying the Chicago of the late Mayor Daley or any other machine politician of the present era. He notes the sociological function the machine and the party performed for the faithful:

> The political machine is in fact an attempt to maintain, inside the formal administrative organization of the city, the control of a primary group. The organizations thus built up, of which Tammany Hall is the classic illustration, appear to be thoroughly feudal in their character. The relations between the boss and his ward captain seem to be precisely that of personal loyalty on the one side and personal protection on the other, which the feudal relation implies.[11]

And he proposed a complete program for the political sociology of cities focusing on the study of the urban power structure.[12] In this area of research, as in the others above, Park was not alone, of course. But he was a demon in getting this kind of research going. And in general, Park was a founder. Soon after publication of his key article, sociologists everywhere were asking his questions.

Each of Park's areas of inquiry- the neighborhood, the city as a mosaic of groups, and urban, or local, politics—is an area of active research in sociology. We will take each up in turn.

The Neighborhood: A Loyalty to Place

Loyalty to "the old neighborhood" is a complex emotion for millions of older Americans. Either they have memories of an intimate urban or rural environment, or they have parents and grandparents who can tell them what life was like in their own old neighborhood long ago. Nostalgia often softens the difficulties that were experienced or blots them out completely. Urban slum landlords, for example, were not invented in our time. They were in business a century ago. Then as now, profit could be gathered by keeping rents high, people crammed in, and services poor. But life went on in spite of such pressures and in some ways, as Park noticed, because of the pressures. The social organization of the neighborhood, starting out for defensive reasons, became with time a web of group friendships in a new home.

For the usually middle-class sociologists of the early days, poor neighborhoods were a kind of foreign land, an uncharted area to be investigated with the new questions of community sociology. One classic study can serve as an introduction to looking at communities sociologically—William Foote Whyte's *Street Corner Society*.[13] Learning something of who Whyte was, what he tried to do, what he found, and what it means today can give us one-case introduction to the aims, methods, and problems of community sociology.

The story takes place in an Italian neighborhood of Boston, the North End, in the late 1930s. Whyte was a graduate student at Harvard, with a fellowship that allowed him to use his time any way he wished. He was new to sociology, new to field research, and young and inexperienced generally. He got on the subway in Harvard Square in Cambridge and went to "Cornerville." On arrival he tried to meet some young women living in the neighborhood:

> The approach seemed at least as plausible as anything I had been able to think of. I resolved to try it out. I picked on the Regal Hotel, which was on the edge of Cornerville. With some trepidation I climbed the stairs to the bar and entertainment area and looked around. There I encountered a situation for which my adviser had not prepared me. There were women present all right, but none of them was alone. Some were there in couples, and there were two or three pairs of women together. I pondered this situation briefly, I had little confidence in my skill at picking up one female, and it seemed inadvisable to tackle two at the same time.
>
> Still, I was determined not to admit defeat without a struggle. I looked around me again and now noticed a threesome: one man and two women. I approached this group and opened with something like this: "Pardon me. Would you mind if I joined you?" There was a moment of silence while the man stared at me. He then offered to throw me down the stairs. I assured him that this would not be necessary and demonstrated as much by walking right out of there without any assistance.[14]

It turned out that Cornerville people didn't go to the Regal Hotel; they were not welcome there. But that wasn't what hurt, of course.

All field studies, in other words, have false starts, and all community researchers make mistakes. Learning from people like Whyte, who have been honest and open enough to tell what theirs were, later researchers have been able to develop more effective techniques for establishing themselves in the field. Whyte was luckier next time around, for he met Doc, who became one of his best informants. Doc was intelligent, had a wide circle of friends, was an excellent amateur

sociologist in his own right, and understood Whyte's aim of writing
a book about the neighborhood—even before Whyte did, apparently.
Whyte then decided to rent a room in the North End, to study Italian
from language records, and to participate in the life of the neighborhood. One of the main things he did was hang out on the corner with
Doc and his club, informal or gang, who called themselves "the
Nortons." The family he rented a room from, whose name was Martini, adopted him. Papa Martini corrected his Italian (which he didn't
really need much, but which convinced many of his sincerity).
Whyte helped out once in a while in the Martini family's restaurant
downstairs from the apartment. He sums up:

> Though I made several useful contacts in the restaurant or through the
> family, it was not for this that the Martinis were important to me. There
> is a strain in doing such work. The strain is greatest when you are a
> stranger and are constantly wondering whether people are going to accept
> you. But, much as you enjoy your work, as long as you are observing and
> interviewing, you have a role to play, and you are not completely relaxed.
> It was a wonderful feeling at the end of a day's work to be able to come
> home and relax and enjoy myself with the family. Probably it would have
> been impossible for me to carry on such a concentrated study of Corner-
> ville if I had not had such a home from which to go out and to which I
> might return.[15]

Whyte got involved with the daily life of Doc's club, the Nortons.
Whyte called them "corner boys," to distinguish them from another
group of Italian-American youths who wanted to get out of the old
neighborhood as quickly as possible. Whyte and the Nortons scorn-
fully called this other group "the college boys." (Note that Whyte,
a real college boy if there ever was one, had become identified with
the corner boys.) Settlement houses, at one of which Whyte met Doc
originally, were one main focus for action. A second, more important
one was club-based sports, such as bowling and baseball. Whyte
began to notice that who won and lost at these games had a lot to
do with their status within the group, the gang. Somehow the group
leaders kept winning more than their skill seemed to indicate they
should. *Informal group rules,* or group norms, were at work here; the
rules held the group together and established the pecking order,
giving a place at the top in the middle, or at the bottom to each
member.[16]

And there was gambling—so much and by so many that it was a

major recreational activity in Cornerville. Tony Cataldo and a few others Whyte got to know introduced him to the world of small-time hoods, paid-off policemen, and organized crime in Cornerville. Whyte soon had to confront his own upbringing and his own previous ideas about breaking the law. To gamble was illegal, but everyone including grandmothers did it, and there he was, taking field notes and even doing a tiny amount of gambling himself. His ties to the community, to Doc, and to the Martini family prevented him from getting kicked down the stairs again, this time for suspicion of spying for the police—the issue just didn't come up. In this way, Whyte came to see that the perceiving of legality and illegality depended on the subgroup in the city doing the perceiving. Cornerville Italians had always gambled in their villages in Italy and felt it was an important social event. The small-time numbers runners and game-parlor operators, who paid their receipts in turn to the Cosa Nostra of the time, were considered legitimate community members. Gambling offered part-time employment to corner boys—running numbers slips. It even offered a chance at occupational success—a career in the rackets—in an economic depression in a pre-World War II American society that bore great prejudice against Italians. Whyte began to discover that a neighborhood's "mores" were not broken down, just because they differed from those of the wider community. Where Park tended to see breakdown Whyte found different standards, tight community organization, and defense against the primarily Irish police and mayor's office. He wound up with a chapter called "The Social Structure of Racketeering."[17]

Another way of looking at what Whyte found is summed up in the sociological concept of *deviance*, which can be defined only in terms of the group and the rules of the group to which it refers. That is, the Cornerville boys and the rackets were not deviant from the point of view of Cornerville itself, but such people and activities were deviant when referred to the wider society, especially as these rules were codified in the laws of Boston and the United States. Depending on where you are, therefore, your actions may be defined either as deviant or conformist—adhering to the same values as your definers. What matters sociologically is who is doing the defining!

Whyte got involved in politics as well. He decided that in this way he could observe the relationships Cornerville had with the rest of Boston. George Revello, a Cornerville boy with no local opposition but with a poor chance to win a city-wide council seat, was the man he worked for. Going to rallies and doing political work gave Whyte an opportunity to see the ways in which the local branch of the Mafia and the local political officers worked hand in hand in the North End. They worked together to assure that everyone who got elected was approved by the racketeers, indebted to them, and thus would act to protect their interests. Whyte, still an outsider in some respects, was also expected in good old Boston political tradition, to "do his duty" by stuffing the ballot box for the North End candidate. In the immortial words of another pol of the time, the late Mayor Curley of Boston, "Vote often, and early, for James Michael Curley!" (Under a series of false names, of course.)

The political process as it operated in many major cities at the time was clearly displayed by this kind of research—for instance, the routine way the police were bought off from watching too closely at the polls.[18] Deviance, then, becomes a problem when it becomes so widely shared that approaches conformity—is it still deviance? Actually, both groups are conforming—Cornerville to its values, the wide city to its own different set of rules (a set which *supposedly* the police and court enforce). Another example was the widespread breaking of the law against drinking during the Prohibition era. Technically the vast majority of drinkers were law-breakers and deviant, but sociologically they were conforming to very widely shared group norms approving drinking. Finally the law had to be repealed to bring it back into line with group norms about drinking. In Whyte's case, observing the deviant behavior and writing it all down caused no end of possible problems, including the life-and-death one of what the mob might think about the results. This is a classic field research problem for sociologists in many situations.

Whyte wrote his book almost as a novel. Names, real people, and lively personalities make the book live even today. The North End has changed some since he wrote, and two more generations have been born. We are no longer in the thirties. The present attorney general of Massachusetts and a former governor of the state have Italian roots. Yet the approach, the models of the group in action, the intertwining of the illegal and legal worlds, the neighborhood as a protective organization against the hostile city—these are still issues. Whyte summed up his experience and his findings by explaining that he built his picture of the neighborhood through personalities on purpose. By following people through time, he constructed a pattern out of person-to-person links:

> Although I could not cover all of Cornerville, I was building up the structure and functioning of the community through intensive examination of some of its parts—*in action.* I was relating the parts together through observing events between groups and between group leaders and the members of the larger institutional structures (of politics and the rackets). I was seeking to build a sociology based upon observed interpersonal events. That, to me, is the chief methodological and theoretical meaning of *Street Corner Society.* [19]

The Community as a Social Mosaic

Investigating the life of a community involves choosing a set of things to look for and an order in which the research should take place. Since very few communities, including small ones, are made up of just one kind of person or group, the way the elements of a community are put together socially should be a high-priority item. But where to begin? A hint from Park—that cities have natural areas —was taken up by urban planners and architects; one such planner has developed a way of mapping the visual areas of a city. It's a good place to start. Then we will review a series of community studies, done in different kinds of neighborhoods and in different places in the urban-to-rural spectrum, to find out how social areas correspond to visual areas. In each case these researchers asked some of Park's original questions about the impact of the city on intimate social life and on group values. Though not all focused on crime, most looked at the issue of social disorganization. They wanted to know the degree to which an area, or the city as a whole, was coming apart at the seams, and disagreeing about the social norms that organize everyday life. One issue here deserves special attention—the heating up of ethnic-neighborhood politics in recent decades, which some sociologist call the "melting-pot debate." Then we will take up the new phenomena of neighborhood renewal and the move back from the suburbs to the central city.

No simple introduction can do justice to the complex nature of community life or the depth and detail of the classic studies we touch on here. But that is the community for you—a tremendously complex mosaic, but *not* a mosaic set in stone; ever-changing patterns mean we always come new to the sociology of a community, even one that has been studied for years.

Community Image: The Eye as Map Maker

Kevin Lynch, an urban planning professor, has a way of sensitizing students to the city as an expereince. He gives students a set of visual elements to look for, a set of things that the urban environment does to the eye, and says, "Go out and map this town or city where you are at school." What, for example, are the *visual boundaries* of a city district? Are they the water's edge by a river, a half-mile-long railroad embankment, a row of twenty-story office buildings rising behind a neighborhood of two-story homes, a shopping center on the edge of a prairie that goes on in wheat for as far as the eye can see? Does a large superhighway cut two parts of the city in half, as happens in parts of Boston and Detroit and in Los Angeles? Where are the primary *paths* for people, along which the eye also travels? In Boston a main one is Commonwealth Avenue, a broad avenue with a park down the center, with five-story trees; in Denver, a main one is the road heading to the wall of the Rockies.

Next, what are the natural or man-made *landmarks*, the locations that people can see or think of as markers for an area of the city? The gold dome of the State House in Boston, the Centennial Arch in St. Louis along the Mississippi, the Mormon Tabernacle in Salt Lake City, the Watts Tower in the Watts section of Los Angeles—these are visually strong targets people use to to give one another directions. In rural areas there are landmarks too, of course. No area is really without them, though some are far more famous than others.

Two more concepts are helpful in mapping the visual image of a community. *Nodes* are points of great activity. These people hangouts, such as a traffic circle, or the chain of little urban parks in downtown Savannah, Georgia, can be marked on your map as small circles. Finally, there are the *visual districts* of the city. I immediately think of three very different areas of New Orleans: the French Quarter, the Garden District, and the business district around the Superdome. Districts are areas that one knows by sight, sound, and feel (even smell, sometimes) after one has spent time in them. They have some identifying visual characteristic, such as the lacy iron grillwork of the porches of the French Quarter or the long, tropical avenue of

St. Charles Street in the Garden District, to take two areas of New Orleans. Every city has them—in Boston I think of the bow-front brick houses on Beacon Hill and in the Back Bay, or the great Neon Row of Las Vegas, or the old sections of San Antonio and Montreal. So too for every square with an old wood bandstand, at the center of little towns and small cities in the nation.

Some interesting sociological questions can be asked after a visual map of this kind is made. First, if a group of people make individual maps, the map may not agree exactly, because the city means different things for different people. New York magazine, for example, asked painters, ballet dancers, and stockbrokers to make sketch maps of Manhattan.[20, 21] They highlighted different features, the ones they cared about. Another question is whether a district is stereotyped socially as Harlem has become, or lower Park Avenue is, to take two areas of New York City. Does the architecture really tell all? It didn't in the North End of Boston, which outwardly had the look of a brick-tenement slum. But within, most apartments were clean, bright, and well taken care of. The stores were crowded and cluttered but clean and lively.

Finally, what physical boundaries limit an area? Do physical barriers create social differences, no man's lands? Do people begin to forget about the part of town on the other side of the superhighway? What's it like to live there?

In general, the visual mapping of a city provides a background for sociological research proper. Relationships between the physical environment and social activities are critically important. A quick map is one way to get started, but it is only a first step. A lot of time needs to be spent in a place if you are to be sure about what is happening socially.

Areas: From Ghetto Street Corner to Rural Hamlet

One way to get a feeling for the ways sociologists investigate community life is to review some classic community studies. We'll begin with the poorest, black ghetto area of a major city, then move through other areas, climbing the social-class ladder as we go away from downtown until finally we leave the city altogether. In each study two issues were almost always covered. These were the impact of the immediate social environment on personal relationships, attitudes, and values, and the degree of social organization or disorganization within the study area, including the degree to which it was cut off from the wider society.

Tally's Corner, by Elliot Liebow, studied street-corner life in the black ghetto of Washington, D.C., in the early sixties. Liebow was working very much as Whyte did in the North End, trying to get a feel for life at the bottom, among the unemployed black school dropouts and unwed fathers. They lived in the most run-down section of the city, in the midst of a society that cared very little for them. Liebow found a sort of bonding between the men, even here. But with it went a fear of relationships to women and family life, because the men knew that they could not economically support such a life. (Liebow doesn't stress it, but an element in such situations has been rules in welfare departments that prevent men from living with their wives and children, because to do so could disqualify the women from a major kind of welfare support.) The casual, menial, and irregular work the men were offered, when they were "lucky," did not make them feel much better. They conveyed a great sense of social isolation to Liebow. They felt cut off from close personal relationships—often replacing these with drugs and alcohol. In the city, they felt cut off from respectable black and white working-class areas, by economic barriers and by the barrier of white racism.[22]

Two nearby neighborhoods were studied in Boston. Whyte studied the North End for *Street Corner Society,* and thirty years later Herbert Gans studied the West End for *Urban Villagers.* With some minor changes, it is as if thirty years had not passed. Both Whyte and Gans were interested in the contrast between the "slum-like" visual image of the areas they studied—three- and four-decker brick tenements, laundry on the line, sometimes garbage in the alleys—and the rather close-knit community groups and subgroups they found, the true social organization that lay underneath the visual appearance. Socially there were some critical differences between the two areas. Whyte's 1930s North End was all-Italian and more thoroughly organized politically than the West End of the 1960s. Second, the generation left in the West End in 1960 were there after the migration of more successful ethnics to the suburbs. Some of these people were quite old, or were the less successful ones, in an era without the blocks against "hyphenated" Americans. By the 1960s there were also vacant buildings and open spaces, in the West End. A mayor and an urban renewal expert who believed in razing whole neighborhoods to the ground had targeted the area for demolition. The various ethnic groups, especially Italians, Slavs, and Jews, wanted to hang on. They shared a need for low-rent apartments, and they clustered their lives around the little mom-and-pop stores their friends ran.[23]

Urban renewal, when it came, devastated many of their lives as well as their neighborhood. The people were driven into sections of Boston where no one knew them. There they had to pay rents they couldn't afford for smaller apartments than the ones they had to leave. Small store owners went on welfare; so did many of their customers. The psychological results were grim. Follow-up studies found the rate of hospitalization for mental illness and the rate of dependence on welfare skyrocketing as a consequence of the destruction.[24] One man, a barber in his early sixties, commented:

> I'm not afraid to die, but I don't want to. But if they tear the West End down and we are all scattered from all the people I know and that know me, and they wouldn't know where I was, I wouldn't want to die and people not know it.[25]

This sense of community is what sociologists have always been interested in in such studies—what causes it and what happens when it changes or is destroyed.

More recently the sense of community has become involved with highly emotional issues such as ethnic pride and racism, and the results have become controversial among sociologists and also in the wider society. Nathan Glazer and Daniel Moynihan studied mid-sixties New York in *Beyond the Melting Pot: The Negroes, Puerto Ricans, Jews, Italians, and Irish of New York City.*[26] An attempt by several earlier generations of schoolteachers and public organizations to push the ideology of the "melting pot" did not work— what was in the pot did not melt. After a while people began to prize their differences. Underneath the rhetoric of ethnic rights stood neighborhood politics. In some large cities, such as Chicago, the original ethnic mosaic of a half century ago was still quite remarkably intact in the 1960s. But the groups had not done equally well, and racial lines were stronger than ethnic ones. White ethnic groups, especially the Jews, had used the school systems for upward mobility, to leave the city proper. The Irish in New York and Boston sought a niche in public-sector jobs, such as the police force and civil service. The blacks and Puerto Ricans came to the city later, in a period of high-unemployment and an era demanding more skills than many of them possessed. But the school systems had become disorganized and run down by this time, and were not usable for boosting people. In fact there was open racism among many teachers. The authors found little sympathy on the part of the older ethnic groups for the new arrivals, and much resistance to their moving into the neighborhood. This enmity and hatred of one group for another was to explode into the urban violence of the late sixties. The violence in turn was to lead to a backlash of vindictiveness against the black urban poor and yet more white outmigration away from the decaying city core.

Our next step is out into the mass-produced working-class suburbs to Levittown, studied by Gans in the mid-sixties. He recorded his study in *The Levittowners,* published in 1967. Gans and his family bought a house just like a hundred others. The family lived in it for two years and joined community groups. Gans felt sympathy for the people there. They were people who had been dumped on and looked down by richer urban intellectuals as "Archie Bunker types". He found that all the houses did look alike but that people tried to fix them up and apply little decorative touches to them. Gans observed that these were white middle-class and working-class ethnics who were now in a "melting pot" situation for the first time. Many missed the informal social life and closeness of their old neighborhoods—the sense of community—but they had chosen deliberately to leave these places. Many stated that they were fleeing the influx of blacks into their old neighborhood. They said they feared the crime rate and the urban decay that they felt were sure to follow.[27]

Conformity—acceptance of the prevailing local group norms, values, and culture—was a subject of much interest to Gans in his Levittown study. Conformity did not come only from social pressure. In some cases people were willing and sought to conform. They copied one another out of interest and admiration rather than competitively. All were learning the new middle-class life style from one another. Gans found that the adolescents were bored by the life in the all-residential bedroom community. The adults were irked by the lack of privacy. No fences were allowed between houses, which were quite close together. Yet the break had been made, and the bridges were burned. Very few people here wanted to return to city life, even for night life. The narrowing down of social view that this implies and for many their closeness to debt, left most of them struggling to hang on, afraid of change, angry and fearful about any rise in taxes, cutback in town services, or moving in by strangers, especially blacks.[28]

There is a clear difference between standard and luxury suburbs. You can see it. An upper-middle class professional and executive suburb with its wide lawns and big houses is, for many Americans, the visual image of success. For example, when you drive through Shaker Heights, Ohio, Glencoe, Illinois, Webster Groves, Missouri, or Beverly Hills, California, you *know* where you are. In *Crestwood Heights*, Seeley, Sim and Loosely reported on their study of a Toronto equivalent.[29] They paid special attention to the socialization of children, the role of the school, mental health and family relationships, and the overall attitudes and values of the "winners" who lived there. What they found was not entirely what they had expected. They found, for example, much hidden turmoil. There was a tremendous gap between the world of the hard-driving and conservative male executives on one hand and their confused, often frightened and lonely wives on the other. (This study was done in the early sixties, before feminist ideology had touched many upper-middle-class women.) Women acted as if they existed to please their men and make things easy for them, and to go to women's club meetings. Alienation, for both men and women, was just under this surface. Many of these people who had "made it" found that their life seemed empty.

Consumerism was a major theme of life—buying the most fashionable car, furniture, clothes, and so on. That displaying the new stuff, rather than enjoying it (and maybe wearing it out) was often a prime motive in all the buying was clearly symbolized by the number of living rooms he found with clear plastic dust covers on the furniture, just like a showroom. The research team was particularly interested in mental health, and though the school system was well equipped, it did not strike researchers as a particularly sensitive or happy place for children. High-pressure striving and extreme achievement were what teachers required and the students expected. Parents also pushed in this direction, especially because high marks were needed to get into an elite college. The children were often rebellious or, copying from their parents, manipulative, sneaky, and sometimes even ruthless in their attitudes toward one another. The real world, the world of other kinds of urban people of rural life, seemed far away, as if these people of Crestwood Heights were living in a gilded ghetto. In summer their country camps did as good a job of keeping children and adolescents away from people not like themselves as their winter life. In a word, they were in isolation. The authors seemed almost nostalgic for the life that other community analysts had found, in the North End of Boston for example. But their subjects were not—they were preoccupied with the next car and the next party.[30]

To finish our tour, let's get further out toward the country. A lot of people do not live in large cities or even middle-sized ones or suburbs. I don't. Small towns, such as the one I live in, and "almost cities" (about ten to fifteen thousand people) are still numerous—look at any map. How do they relate to the big city perhaps an hour away? And what does life in a small town mean to people in an age of mass transportation, mass communication, and big corporations interested in controlling the economic life of such small towns by placing their branches there?

Arthur Vidich and Joseph Bensman's *Small Town in Mass Society,* reports on one town of this type. They found themselves getting more and more away from a job they had originally been hired to do by Cornell University—a survey study of education and child training in a small town near the university. The town thought of itself as an independent Rock of Gibraltar, an old-time agricultural community in a corrupt world of big cities. This turned out to be very much of a fiction when the economic dependence of the town on the metropolis was inspected in depth.[31] Vidich and Bensman finally took a "community study" approach that involved depth interviews and a lot of non-quantitative field-study research. This caused problems for their job on the Cornell survey team, but they kept pointing out that the narrow study they had started would not get at the broader issues affecting the town, and thus would cause the narrow issues of education and child rearing to be misunderstood.

Eventually, the Cornell team refused to approve of their work, and the town also rejected them. When the authors finally wrote up the results and had them published, the findings were embarrassing to townspeople, for they showed the many ways in which the town was not in control of its own fate. Vidich and Bensman showed that the town was essentially an economic satellite of the big city. The city made or broke the economy of the town. Thus the small businesses and their owners were not independent of city power; the big shots of the town were in reality small fry.[32] In other words, Vidich and Bensman had punctured the balloon of community pride. Their book sold like hot cakes in town, of course. But on the Fourth of July effigies of the authors were ridden through town on a parade float. They were portrayed in such a way that they appeared to be shoveling manure into the street.[33]

In this trip along the spectrum from city to country and from one class to another, much has not been touched on. For example, we've not explored what made each of these studies unique and made them all art as well as science. But certain themes strike us. In any area of the community, there is some kind of social organization, and yet some disorganization as well. Of course, as Pearl Bailey reports, "I've been rich and I've been poor, and believe me, honey, rich is better." Human problems of coping with the environment and developing a sense of community remain in some ways the same, wherever you are. Yet the degree of isolation or the degree of social togetherness felt in a place—the sense and reality of community—is a subject for sociological community studies at all locations from urban ghetto to small town. Sociology will want to outline the community and understand it dynamically. And the mosaic we describe at one point in time is alive, as we warned, and thus always changing. The bulk of these studies were done in the Fifties and early Sixties. Since then, we have had the War on Poverty, the war in Vietnam, urban riots and protest against racism, backlash, and the cutback of services to the poor. And have also had something else: a reversal of the outward migration from the central city has begun. The rediscovery and rehabilitation of the obsolete urban core is a new and important change. What might it mean sociologically?

Neighborhood Renewal: A Response to the Urban Crisis

As conditions in the cities worsened in the Sixties, out of the chaos and crisis grew government-funded attempts at community action— the OEO Community Action Program and the beginning of rational planning for urban renewal. Then, when both of these attempts began to falter, local, neighborhood-based action by citizen groups increased. These groups fought to turn back the growing disintegration of the central city. Using their own energies instead of government grants, they worked to restore a sense of community. Often they were brought together by an external threat, like the urban renewal program in Boston that demolished the West End. In Baltimore, in the Seventies, one working-class neighborhood was threatened with disintegration when an expressway was scheduled to be built right through it. Gloria Aull led a fight to prevent the city of Baltimore from destroying her neighborhood. She notes:

> Remember, this is definitely a class thing. You never hear of garbage dump in a blue-stocking neighborhood, or of a prison, or an expressway. Its always in the blue-collar neighborhood or the no-collar neighborhood.[34]

Ms. Aull, a housewife, and her group formed a Community Development Corporation to serve as a focus for investment in the neighborhood. She and a social worker (who is now their Congresswoman) organized the Southeast Committee Against the Road (SCAR). The fight was long and bitter, but the road was stopped. Why did they fight? She explains:

> We are very folksy, plain-living, Harry Truman types. Really—our communities are like European villages, whether you go to Greektown, Little Italy, Highlandtown, or Fells Point. And what are we characterized by? First of all, we view the neighborhood as our home, and our neighbors are part of our extended family. Therefore our relationships with our restaurants, our businesses, our candy stores at the corner, are primary relationships. It is the strength of the interpersonal. So that if I'm threatened by an expressway, we all are, and we have a sense of solidarity, and real sense of community because of that. People really love one another, and they love their neighborhood. Their neighborhood is their home.[35]

But what about life in the suburbs? Why are some people beginning to move back to the city, to fight for a turnaround in the economic and social blight, and against the rule of planner-bureaucrats, who had the city to themselves for almost a decade? Ms. Aull again:

> I think people miss the community. They miss having relationships. The American dream that you've got to have those three square yards of grass in front of you has fallen through. People need each other.[36]

Perhaps Ms. Aull has had a course in sociology?

Even if her knowledge is not formal and academic, Aull is an example of a person looking at the world, and her community, sociologically. And she is one who has acted to change its social fabric, consciously and deliberately. There are complicated issues involved here, of course. Not all are unhappy with suburbia, yet it is undeniable that an urban restoration movement is under way and the interest in urban life is attracting more people. Ironically, though, some of the new in-migrants are well-off young professionals who come into a neighborhood and in effect push the working-class residents out. The prices, the rents, and the taxes rise as the neighborhood becomes "stylish." The working class can't afford to stay. For example, Newburyport, Massachusetts declined after its initial period of clipper ships and its industrial revolution, along with the rest of the Merrimac Valley. Since the 1960s it has been undergoing restoration by a lot of prosperous young people moving up from Boston. Newburyport is becoming stylish. There are new boutiques in the old restored brick shopping center. Slowly the old, the poor, and the ethnics of Newburyport are being driven out and pushed over the border to southern New Hampshire.

Another sociological issue raised by the new will of people to organize themselves and get into civic fights involves racism and ethnic prejudice. Organization for one's own group can also be organization against others—against blacks, for example. People and societies are complex. The same neighborhood and ethnic pride that can lead to fixing up a dying Polish neighborhood can also reinforce the will to resist the racial integration of that neighborhood or even to resist the daytime busing of black children into its schools. Yet rehabilitation without such consequences is possible. Chicago's South Shore, a primarily black neighborhood developed by black people, did not lose its remaining white citizens—it even gained a few.[37]

The Christian Science Monitor, in a series on new communities, has called this action "the new localism." They describe it as "a groundswell movement of citizens calling for the return of political and economic power to the local level, largely in response to neglect by big government and failure of such 'top down' solutions as model cities, urban renewal, and the war on poverty."[38] Sociological studies of the new communities in renewal are sure to follow on the heels of all the new local action. Even now they will be trying to provide new answers to the first questions Robert Park asked: What does the community look like as a social system? What are its patterns of social organization and disorganization? How and why are the pieces of the puzzle, the tile in the mosaic, *changing* as we go from one time period to the next? And what does this mean for you? Perhaps we can begin with what it meant for me.

The Fight for Pleasant Valley

Three years ago I became involved in a fight to preserve Pleasant Valley, the beautiful green rural river valley in Batesville, the town in which I live. We were fighting against the creation of a large dump, one that could begin at 30 acres and then, after a while, extend on the top of the hills behind the old houses on the river for almost two miles—a 150 acre dump for the trash and garbage of Boston, Salem, and thirty other cities in eastern Massachusetts. A dump behind *my house.* If created, this dump could ruin a 300-year-old historic area, settled since Puritan times, as well as the unbroken chain of antique country colonial homes built before the American Revolution, that extend ten miles from the old brick mills of Lawrence and Haverhill to the sea at Newburyport. It is one corner of the map, one of a thousand presently threatened by such things. My first ideas (and what was wrong with them), the action of the neighborhood, and the continuing struggle viewed by me sociologically (as against simply as a partisan participant) can serve as a summary of the issues I have raised, and the questions to ask in joining—or perhaps even forming —your own community. Then, after the next chapter on political sociology and political action, we will return again to Pleasant Valley, to review the most recent developments.

Superhighways, as we have observed, can create social as well as visual barriers. A six-lane superhighway cuts the river area of Batesville away from the rest of the town, so that in the eyes of many people in town the river bank is a kind of noman's land. In the early days the Puritan farmers made good use of the rich bottom land of the valley; old engravings show miles of apple orchards on those green hills along the river. In later colonial days sailing ships were built on the flat land by the river bank—my own house was probably built by a shipwright about 1750. But the valley and river really made history in the period of the industral revolution, especially in later years near the turn of the century when Batesville became the Detroit of the East, with its early assembly lines for carriages and then early electric cars. Thousands of French Canadians moved south to work in the Batesville mills, and were miserably exploited economically in the process. The rich lived in one section by the river, the poor workers scattered through the town.

But the town, like many mill towns in the old industrial North, went into decline as industry moved south. By the early 1970s Batesville was suffering from 17 percent unemployment rate, rising taxes, and a squeeze on the income of the primarily working-class population. The old Yankee aristocracy had retired from politics, and almost all offices were in the hands of the French-Canadian ethnic group (sometimes the sons and grandsons of the original immigrants). A lot of people were simply passive, but pressed. Enter the large corporation—in this case the Cleanliness Corporation of America, haulers of trash and garbage on a grand scale, for the entire East Coast, a firm with the ability to hire large corporate law firms whenever it got into legal hot water by not obeying town ordinances. If the town would accept 50 cents a ton for all outsider garbage and trash and get its own trash taken and collected free, would the town allow CCA to use the town as a kind of regional garbage dump? Would Pleasant Valley be a reasonable place for it? The town official huddled. Open hearings were supposed to be held, but most discussions went on behind closed doors. There was no town referendum—but the town was said to be in *favor* of this. Not, of course, the people in Pleasant Valley.

A town's values are not always worn on its sleeve. Batesville has, for example, an excellent school system for its income level, and an outstanding small hospital and a public library with the latest nonfiction and university-press books. It was once beautiful all over, and still areas like Pleasant Valley, where the old beauty remains. But by and large, as I was to find, it did not have my up-from-Boston typical professor values—ecology, historical preservation, zoning, saving the environment. Also, according to older residents, the town was not free of corruption. It was suggested—though no proof was available—that some town officials were in collaboration with the Cleanliness Corporation people. In any case, the main political tradition was that reformers always lose, that the people in Town Hall are able to resist any attempt to influence them.

I became feverish with plans and angry, and my first thoughts were not sociological analysis at all. (Yes, do as I *say*, don't do as I *do*, and yes, sociologists can lose their temper about society too, though not all will share this with students.) Since the Bicentennial was coming, my first idea was a demonstration. Why shouldn't I dress up as Paul Revere and ride a horse into the town Fourth of July picnic crying, "The garbage is coming! The garbage is coming!" The town paper heard about this ahead of time and angrily printed an editorial on how people ought not to ruin the "birthday party of our nation" with "political activities." My God, I thought, so this is what the Revolution means in small towns today. But my values and approaches were obviously out of phase. What then to do? To begin with, understand the social system of Batesville.

A group of valley residents decided that two things needed to happen—the education (or socialization) of the town about the meaning, beauty, and importance of the valley, and the raising of money for a legal battle, against all the town boards if necessary, to prevent their giving the Cleanliness Corporation the permits they needed to begin work. That August we held the first annual Pleasant Valley Day—affair, by the river, to raise money. The events were chosen to be fun, with a few educational handouts and a slide show, which I made, on the history of Pleasant Valley; we put it on free in a barn. We began to be a neighborhood, to develop a sense of community, that Bicentennial summer. The event was a major success— with beer, balloons, games, pony-cart rides, and a gigantic yard-sale flea market. Come to the valley—see that it is too beautiful to ruin. This was the general idea.

People came to the first Pleasant Valley Day, as they have to the next two as well. A few handouts were picked up, and we got some newspaper coverage. But people came to have fun, and we did not get any new converts to our cause. Our battle in the courts has been going on for three years as I write this—is still going on and will still go on. We have finally begun to get some help from the environment people at the state level and some members of our local conservation commission. But the majority of the town does not think of itself as threatened—does not have a concept of the town that includes the valley. On the New Hampshire border there is a strong value— "Don't tell me what to do in my back yard and I won't complain about what happens in yours." There also may be some jealousy of the people who live on the river, mistaking us for the rich. And in comparison to the poor and pinched majority of Batesville, we may seem well-off.

In any case, there is a basic class-conflict problem. For the long-ter:n solution—taking all garbage and trash out of town—will probably cost a little more than having the CCA people turn one section of their town into a dump for the rest of eastern Massachusetts—money they feel they can't afford. And another thing—many old-timers have told me the townspeople have no sense of pride any more, that they don't care. I don't buy this for a minute, since I saw them and helped them fight as a whole united town against an attempt by some state health bureaucrats to take their hospital away. But the environment and beauty issue doesn't work here. We have raised $15,000 but have gotten no one but ourselves to show up for town board meetings, no matter how hard we have tried. But we won't quit.

Was the fight worth it? What did I learn and gain? First, I got an insight into the town's values that simply was not possible by doing a survey. Second, my children got an education in the importance of fighting to preserve the environment. They have been very active in this and other such battles in this area, and we have learned much, I think, from the experience. Third, some town officials finally began to vacillate on their previous, pro-garbage stance. Apparently there have been people elsewhere in town talking quietly to them about the image of the town and its consequences for business. Even before the final year of the fight, to be reported in the next chapter, I had planned to make an appearance at the town businessmen's association on "The Image of Batesville: Its Economic Meaning." And there is even a group hired by the town—an architect from Newburyport with some brick-mill restorers—which was hired at this time to plan the revitalization of Batesville's mills as small electronic firms, shops, and so on. And finally, most important of all, we in the valley now had a sense of community. Two years ago in the Fall, on one of those golden days where people were out raking their leaves, I drove down our bumpy river road, with my left hand out the window. I waved to everyone outside in front—and they all waved back. It felt like home.

Joining Your Community: Now, Not Later

There once was a time when the majority of college students who lived away from home were carefully watch over by the college, which acted *in loco parentis,* in the place of the parent. The college kept them on campus all or most of the time, almost in a sort of prisoner status. Now, even at rural colleges, and certainly at urban and community colleges, the town around the campus is an integral part of the life of the college. You may say you don't have any time to pay attention to that town and its life. You are wrong if that is what you think. But if you do have almost no free time, you need to *make* time. My plea is the same, regardless of where you are in school: *Join your community! Now, not later!* So many people go through life with their eyes on ultimate goals, an eventual home, a never-never land, too busy to look in front of them. The place where they live now and their neighbors—in the dorm or across the street —hardly exist for them. I have known people who have bought groceries at a corner store for ten years without ever reaching out at all to get to know their grocer. I pity them. The sense of community —a sense of belonging—is a possibility, but one that you'll have to develop with others, right where you are now.

Explore your community sociologically. Get to know it first as an aesthetic experience. City-scapes have character; so do small towns, even suburban shopping malls. Get to know the town, not just the "gown," the people on campus. Define for yourself the visual boundaries of your community. Perhaps you might go out on a mapping expedition, as Kevin Lynch did with his students. What are the social and ethnic subgroups in the community and what events are they planning next week? Try the ethnic restaurant shortcut—don't be afraid to ask questions about the Greek community of the owner of the local Greek restaurant. Discover what social networks underlie the city or town's politics. Take some risks, if you live in an area in conflict, in one experiencing change. Find out for yourself what the community controversies are. Read that local community newspaper with this in mind. Get involved and take a stand. Join a group that has values you share, and act in the community political process. At the least you will begin to find the *people* out there, and will feel less like a robot, a peg in an academic slot, a ship passing in the night.

Now a warning—you may not like what you find out there. What *you* think of as conformity, the community may consider deviance, and vice versa. Fine, I expect that too. But a sociological perspective should help you understand the *why* of the action, the norms, and the deviance or conformity of your community and its subgroups to some set of standards and values. Sociological investigations will show you how the community's values line up with, or differ from, your own. Perhaps you may want to change your own, or change theirs. You may fight to do that, and lose, and then move on. The sociological skills of community discovery that you can learn in a longer study of the subject will still hold. If anything, the more you're a newcomer to any area, the more natural it will be for you to become a community sociologist—with or without the formal training. Of course, I'd prefer *with*. . . .

For Further Reading

Robert E. Faris. *Chicago Sociology, 1920–1932.* Chicago: University of Chicago Press, 1970.

The story of urban sociology at Chicago, as well as other new specialties such as social psychology, as sociology developed in one of the first major departments. The setting of Chicago is featured, and biographies are given for each of the early stars of sociology.

William Foote Whyte. *Street Corner Society.* Chicago: University of Chicago Press, 1943.

There is no substitute for the original. The liveliness of this report, the depth of feeling, and the clear writing have few equals. Newer paperback editions have Whyte's later comments on his experience.

Herbert Gans. *The Urban Villagers: Group and Class in the Life of Italian-Americans.* New York: Free Press, 1962.

Herbert Gans. *The Levittowners: Ways of Life and Politics in a New Suburban Community.* New York: Random House, 1967.

The same observer in two very different places, with a group of older ethnics left behind in a failing neighborhood, and with younger ethnics who have moved away to developments where all the houses look alike. Both books are perceptive and sympathetic.

Nathan Glazer and Daniel P. Moynihan. *Beyond the Melting Pot: The Negroes, Puerto Ricans, Jews, Italians, and Irish of New York City.* Cambridge, Mass.: M.I.T. Press, 1970.

Controversial because it named names and punctured myths. A good predictor of the ethnic politics of the seventies. Also good on the tragic lack of sympathy groups have for one another.

Kai Erikson. *Everything in Its Path: Destruction of Community in the Buffalo Creek Flood.* New York: Simon and Schuster, 1976.

A community is reconstructed by people whose homes have been destroyed by a natural disaster with man-made dimensions as well. Politically critical, beautifully written, highly recommended.

Maurice Stein, Arthur J. Vidich, and Joseph E. Bensman (ed.). *Reflections on Community Studies.* New York: Wiley, 1964.

A number of the leading sociological community researchers think back to their time in the host towns—what it felt like to be there, what mistakes were made, how the communities reacted to the studies. Gives good insights into the sociologist at work.

Marc Fried, with Ellen Fitzgerald and others. *The World of the Urban Working Class.* Cambridge, Mass.: Harvard University Press, 1973.

The study of personal destruction of hope and the society's discarding of the people of the West End of Boston. The researchers followed them where they went after their community was leveled and replaced by high-rent apartments for well-to-do Bostonians. Deals with the consequences for mental health of old-style urban renewal, or "people removal."

Albert Hunter, *Symbolic Communities: The Persistence and Change of Chicago's Local Communities.* Chicago: University of Chicago Press, 1974.

Going back to the source and the old maps of Park and Burgess—did the old Chicago neighborhoods survive into the present day? Yes and no. The story, with careful data, on the psychological image of a community as a symbol as well as the fact of numbers.

Rosabeth Moss Kanter. *Commitment and Community: Communes and Utopias in Sociological Perspective.* Cambridge, Mass.: Harvard University Press, 1972.

Some people take to the hills and set up communes. How these work out or don't is the subject of this fascinating study. Alternative styles in community living are discussed sociologically.

Morton Rubin. *The Walls of Acre: Intergroup Relations and Urban Development.* New York: Holt, Rinehart and Winston, 1974.

The story of groups of Arabs, Jews, and Christians who have lived in quarters of this ancient Israeli city for more than 2,000 years. Topical, given the Arab-Israeli conflict, as well as useful for comparing another nation's ethnic mosaics with our own.

Chapter

FIVE

Acting Politically

Act politically? Why bother? Almost everyone has had the feeling that nothing can be done to change a situation. Yet situations change, and sometimes because people acted after all. But what can one person do, or a small group, for that matter? And is it worth the effort? The mass media lately have been full of cheap, quick "historical analysis," saying that the early Eighties are going to be a quiet time, a time of student and general social passiveness, of a return to Fonzieland—to the myth of what the Fifties were (but really weren't.) We are thus encouraged to feel the limits of our own political effectiveness and to conclude that it's no use fighting city hall, or Exxon. Yet if sociology has one message here, it is that *not* acting is a political act all its own—a vote for things as they are.

Why people act or don't act, and what the consequences are for society when they do, have been topics of great importance for sociology since its early years. How sociologists have gone about studying the political world can tell us a lot about what sociology is. And the debates within sociology reflect bigger debates, out there in the world at large. We can begin by returning to the time of childhood and the growing-up process. From our sociological perspective we can ask a narrower range of questions than those we asked earlier in the book: Where do people get their political attitudes and values? How has sociological research advanced in its understanding of political socialization in the past twenty years or so? Next, the issue of

132

citizen participation, not only in voting but in all the other area of politics as well, has been increasingly the focus of the sociologist's attention. What is being learned here, and how does the research progress? Next we will consider the concept of *power* and the social consequences of the exercise of power. How does the *power structure* of a community get set up, and how is it described by sociologists? What models have been invented to grasp this process whole? Then we will move up to the big picture—the national level. Especially important here is one debate that continues to rage not within sociology but also within our society as a whole: What is the real power of the giant corporations and what does this power mean in a democratic society? Would a change to a noncapitalist society change what is done in our country about individual rights, wealth and its distribution, human services for those in need? What debates at the level of social theories describe this worldwide conflict cover up, or highlight, this kind of problem? How do the competing theories do in terms of finding supporters and enemies within the world of academia, the main haunt of most sociologists? Finally, we will return to the Pleasant Valley fight, to see what has happened in the year since the events described in the last chapter, as they help to illustrate political issues from a sociological point of view.

On Becoming Political: Research in Progress

In discussing how we become social creatures, in Chapter 1, "Discovering Yourself" I left out a key element because of its central relevance here. It is the process by which political values and attitudes are conveyed from one generation to the next by the society at large, by mass media, and by family and friends. This aspect of socialization and research on it go by the name *political socialization*. Its a key to learning how and why a society stays the same or goes into spasm and revolution.

We can begin with the limited question Why do people vote as they do? About twenty years ago the first answers to this question entered the research literature of sociology. Reports cropped up in the articles in professional journals and the papers given at regional and national meetings. At that time it seemed as if political-party membership and especially whether one voted Democratic or Republican were usually "inherited" socially—people voted the same as their parents. In other words, it seemed that parents socialized their children *here* as everywhere else.

In these early studies, the vast majority of parents voting for Democratic candidates seemed to produce Democratic-voting children, and Republican voters produced Republican voters.[1] Not surprising, was the conclusion, for who else had such a long time to influence a person in all areas of attitudes about life and government? But the difference between research and "common sense" is that research doesn't quit. Any finding is simply a step on the way to more complete findings, to newer and what is hoped will be better information. Some sociologists and political scientists noted that voting is only one kind of political activity. What about sit-ins and demonstrations for civil rights, against a war, against abortion, against welfare cutbacks? Did *these* kinds of political activity get learned at home? And what about the children who later didn't follow in their parents' voting footsteps? What or who influenced *them*?

More questions arose. By the early Seventies there were some older sociologists who had done research on, and lived through, the Fifties, the Sixties, and the early Seventies.[2] It struck them that when a person hit maturity might make a difference. Was there an important difference for one's politics between being a teenager when Eisenhower was on television and growing up in a time when the images of the antiwar movement were flashing on the screen month after month? Or when the impeachment proceedings against President Nixon were getting under way? Can the point in history at which you form your opinions have an effect on those opinions quite aside from parental influence? And what about your *own* ideas? If adolescence is a time when parents' values and ideas are questioned, doesn't this lead junior high, high school, and college students to turn to their friends to ask what *they* think about acting, or not acting, politically?

Every question of this kind is really a proposal for a research project. Find a group of young adults and interview them on their political behavior—not just voting, but other kinds of activity too. Then ask questions about their parents. Did they come from a wealthy family? In wealthy families, politics are often a prime topic of conversation. Moreover, they may be talked about in such a way that a child learned, for instance, that when Daddy got mad he called the Governor, and the Governor not only listened but *did something* about what Daddy told him. Or was the family poor? Was politics a sad grumble over a plate of beans, a beaten welfare mother answering her child's question with something like "They don't really do anything for us, honey, except make promises at election time, and they certainly wouldn't listen if I wrote a letter." So our imaginary research project needs questions on the occupation, if any, of the parents, their income and where they lived, and their political activity or lack of it. Then it becomes possible to see what in the political behavior of parents is related to what in the political behavior of their children. For comparison purposes do this for research subjects of different ages—say one group who were teenagers in the mid-Fifties, one that hit adolescence in the middle Sixties, and a group just now graduating from high school

If this study sounds like it is beginning to get complicated and expensive in addition, well, of course it is. But the real world is complicated, especially if you really want to take into account all the influences on people over the twenty years or so it took them to reach maturity. But we really *do* need such studies. This kind of research is only now beginning to get done.

In one extensive research report on the political character of adolescence, Kent Jennings and Richard Niemi concluded this way:

> Taking into account all family and school factors by no means accounts in full for the political dispositions of eighteen-year-olds. There is much in their political profiles that cannot be explained by direct appeal to the principal agents of learning.[3]

Three reasons were given for these findings. First was the number of different sources of ideas on politics, including parents, relatives, teachers, television coverage political action, and personal experience. Second, not too many families deliberately school their children in voting behavior. Third was the issue of the historical period, again as experienced directly and through television coverage of events in the period. Finally, Jennings and Niemi recognized something sociologists sometimes forget, that we are individuals and can make up our own minds in spite of social pressures. By the time of voting age but often far earlier, we have begun to develop what Jennings and Niemi call a "political self":

Even in the very earliest stages of political life the child is not simply a reflecting glass which mirrors the image of others. Rather, the child's own needs and drives, mental and physical endowments, and evolving cognitive structure vitally influence the way in which political stimuli are initially interpreted and absorbed and later are sought out and used.[4]

Some of you may remember the way families were torn apart about the legitimacy of the fight against the war in Vietnam. It was often fathers and mothers against their older children. All those arguments could never have happened if political learning were automatic and came straight from parents. History, in the guise of the actions of a series of presidents, intruded on the usually more peaceful orbit of family political discussions.

Even tracing one social characteristic, or variable, over a period of time can tell us interesting things that make the social picture more complex than we originally thought but also make our understanding of political socialization deeper. From the Thirties to the Fifties women showed up in the research findings as much less active politically than men. They voted less and were less informed about politics. If they were married, they tended to ask their husbands how they should vote. By the mid-Sixties however, the findings were changing. The differences between men and women were diminishing. By the early Seventies they were effectively gone. Anyone want to guess why? In general, such one-item studies and the more broadly based research by such workers as Jennings and Niemi are slowly building a surer understanding of the complex ways that growing up both *determines* our attitudes and frees us from attitudes that we may have had earlier in life.

To understand the research approach to a social process, we have to consider the unknown along with the known—the uncharted territory. One huge area is missing from what I've said so far: the nature and extent of political influence by the mass media. Liberals and conservatives argue in the pages of *TV Guide* and elsewhere that TV news is "too liberal." Other critics of the mass media observe that NBC, CBS, and ABC are themselves giant corporations or even owned in turn by other larger corporations. They add that this ownership drastically restricts what can be said on television about the political influences these corporations have on all major decisions.[5] Is the news slanted? Who says so? Who disagrees? And so what?

Does it have much impact on people's thinking, slanted or not? This is such a controversial area and so threatening to some interests with money that it is hard to get research support for the major studies that will be necessary to find out more. One thing is certain, though. Totalitarian societies are convinced that the media are important in influencing political opinion. If they weren't convinced of this I doubt they would totally censor the media in their characteristic way.

Citizen Participation: Questions, Answers, More Questions

For many years one of Johnny Carson's main roles has been that of Karnak the Magnificent, a mystical, turbaned, flea-brained fortuneteller. Ed McMahon, Carson's straight man, feeds the great Karnak answers. The trick is can swami think up the question? One of the first problems of a sociologist is to decide what questions to ask. This problem in turn brings up an even more basic one, defining what the *topic* is going to be on which the questions will be asked. Ask a broad question on a broad topic and a whole range of ways can be found to answer it. A narrower question can be answered only in more restricted ways. On the other hand, that more carefully limited question may be easier to answer, and people may be surer of the answer when it is produced. Almost all sociologists go through a procedure of defining their research when they plan it, no matter what style of research they use. "Citizen participation"—the varieties of citizen action by those who have come of age and begun to act politically—is a useful topic for showing how this process takes place. First, there is the problem of defining the term. What precisely are we going to mean by citizen participation? (The "we" here by the way, is the researcher, who makes up the definition and then must share it with us or be accused of deliberate fuzziness.) Second, how big a piece of the topic pie is going to be bitten off? One kind of participation studied in one place during one year? A broad social movement studied over fifty years? And then what is the *aim* of the research? Next, what *indexes,* or measure, of participation will we use? Finally, after the data are analyzed, what are the findings and what do they mean not only for more research but also for political action?

In the centuries before sociology came on the scene, there were still plenty of observers of the social life of those times, and some made general statements about issues and roles for participation in political life. In the Middle Ages, for example, a person was defined by the church and the king as a subject, not a citizen. Being a subject meant you did not have any civil rights except those that the king had temporarily granted to you with the approval of the church. The Enlightenment gave birth to a new idea during the century that led up to the American and French revolutions. Social philosophers suggested that people were born with "certain inalienable rights," civil rights of free speech and ownership of property that no one, especially no king, could take away. A new term, "citizen," was coined.[6]

Post-Revolutionary America was an experiment—a nation of citizens instead of subjects, without a hereditary aristocracy. What were the citizens to do politically? The years between our success at gaining independence from England and the time of the Constitutional Convention of 1789 were devoted to defining this role. The debate was fierce, with some working to narrowly restrict citizen rights, especially the vote, others trying to widen them. (No one planned to give the right to vote, to slaves or women, of course, or to those who didn't own any land.) A compromise between the two factions was reached by establishing a narrow category of people able to vote. The next two centuries would have as one theme the fight by one or another originally excluded group to get the right of citizen participation through voting.[7]

From the start it was realized that voting was not the only way to be politically powerful. For example, the owners of plantations and ships early developed ways of circumventing this kind of participation if its results were not going in the direction they wanted. They bought what they wanted through bribery or threat of reprisal if votes went against them. By the time modern sociological research on citizen participation began, a real problem of defining it existed. Some equated participation with voting alone; others had a broader definition. But almost all sociologists were just looking at isolated individuals. A more accurate definition, I think, was recently proposed by Robert Alford and Roger Friedland, of "political participation," a term including groups participating as well as individual citizens:

> We regard political participation as those present *or past* activities by private citizens and *private or public organizations and groups,* that are more

or less directly aimed at influencing the selection of governmental *structures and personnel,* and *influencing* the actions they take *or do not take.*[8]

Note the italics in their definition. In reviewing hundreds of previous studies, they became concerned that almost all were *voting* studies of *individuals,* rather than studies of lobbying and pressures by organized groups. Also, their definition reminds us that the aim of participation may not necessarily be to elect someone, but rather to change a bureaucracy or to stop a project (such as Aull's fight against the freeway or Pleasant Valley against the dump.) In making this broader definition they were proposing a broader program of future research on participation. They feared that research in the past had ignored some of the most important areas of all. Then they went on to note that the research findings already in were challenging a major myth—that participation means power. Not necessarily, they said, for powerful corporations often work behind the scenes or simply sit there and are consulted ahead of time *before* a president makes a move. Even more surprising to Alford and Friedland, given the extent of the myth, no studies have been done that precisely measure the impact voting really has on decisions by government. This goes especially for the poor and working class. In summary, Alford and Friedland observe:

> The forms of participation in non-party, non-legislative institutions by the poor and working classes have very little impact on the structure and policies of those institutions and ultimately little effect upon the conditions of their lives . . . political participation by the poor has the effect of siphoning off political leadership into ineffective channels, thus preventing political challenge of the dominant economic institutions of the society. The function, if not the intention, of those forms of participation is to control or limit the consequences of that participation. This is participation *without* power.[9]

Note the further questions this statement raises. First, the big one —how true is their conclusion? Then, in detail, what kinds of participation are carried out by whom, attempting to change what? And in each kind of attempt, what is the picture of success and failure? There are many ways to try to answer these questions from the narrow to the broad. For example, let's briefly review these four ways: studies relating people's social characteristics, especially their income level, to whether they vote in elections; studies classifying participation into different kinds of activity and then asking who engages in what kind; studies that attempt to see what finally happens when a group of citizens participate in a government program that has a board or panel set up for their input; and finally, broad-scale, historical studies of entire political movements. Each is a type of research on participation.

The pioneering studies in the area of citizen participation looked at voting behavior—who voted and who didn't in local, state, and national elections. People were classified by their social characteristics—race, age, sex, and especially income level and other measures of "socioeconomic status." Study after study found the upper and upper middle class voting more frequently in all kinds of elections than the working class, and they voted in turn far more than the poor. Different conclusions were drawn from these findings. Some social scientists thought that the poor had given up on the system, and should thus be encouraged to vote to make their voices heard. Other researchers said that because the poor had voted in the past and it hadn't done any good, they had stopped, and were now getting involved in more direct action. Note that unless you look at other forms of participation, you can't even begin to see which explanation is closer to the truth.

A second area of studies looked at *types* of participation. Two studies did survey this broader field of participation; they were the groundbreakers about ten years ago. One, by Sidney Verba and N.H. Nie, studied a large sample of the American population. The study found that in addition to the extremes of very active people who participated both in voting and non-voting activities, and the totally passive people, there were two kinds of middle-level actors. The first kind were active on local issues, such as ecology battles and anti-expressway fights, but ignored formal party politics. The second kind worked for local and state political candidates, but not in community action fights.[10] Lester Milbrath, another researcher, reviewed all the studies done before him and created a spectrum from "spectator" at one end to "gladiator" at the other.[11] Verba and Nie and Milbrath agreed in one critical way: regardless of the activity, voting or campaigning, fighting dumps or freeways, the poor were less active than the working class, and they less active than the wealthy.

But even though the field of study is now wider, the results of participation are not yet under consideration. This study area grew in importance in the Sixties. A natural experiment was created by government programs of the mid-Sixties, set up to answer demands by the poor that they be allowed to have an impact on policies affecting their lives. The requests for an increase in "citizen participation" led to the next question—what results did the citizens get by participation on boards of community action programs? In this area I did some work myself, both by reviewing the literature and by acting as a consultant to the technical assistance division of the Community Action Program of OEO. I flew in and out of a number of cities and made short but intensive inspections of the OEO citizen participation process, and I reviewed what others had written about the subject. I came to realize that rubber-stamp participation was really what had been set up by the government program—the poor were supposed to automatically approve the decisions already made by the program professionals. In city after city, when the poor actually started pushing the action agency, the upper-level bureaucracies (Washington OEO headquarters) reacted nervously and local politicians reacted angrily. The action was embarrassing to them. Yet when the citizens were passive, they got nothing out of the program.[12]

Other observers of the program, and of similar programs such as the Model Cities program, found that the claims made for participation were far higher than the reality. Five years later Alford and Friedland summarized the evidence that there was a clear distinction between citizen participation in government programs and citizen power over them, and that *participation without power* was highly characteristic of the experience of many Americans, and not just the poor.

But even these studies were localized. They did not look at the big picture, or at long-term historical changes. They focused on one time period (especially on the late Sixties) and ignored the great social movements of poorer people in recent American history—the union movement, the civil rights movement, the welfare rights movement. These movements constituted an area that cried out for historical research with a sociological perspective, especially on the impact of the poor and working class as social actors in attempting to change their society through direct action. With experience as participants as well researchers, Frances Fox Piven and Richard Cloward have recently written a broad-scale, historical analysis of the action of the working class and the poor in these movements. Their conclusions about what was effective and what was ineffective were startling, but not surprising in the light of all these previous studies: The working class and the poor have gotten support, wages, and goods only with the threat of violence and the carrying out of social disruption. Voting has never gotten the gains that were promised for groups struggling for it, and carefully prearranged government programs with a built-in slot for "participation" have failed too. The main conclusion of Piven and Cloward's book, *Poor People's Movements: Why They Succeed, How They Fail,* is this:

> Elites respond to the institutional disruptions that protest causes, as well as to other powerful institutional imperatives. Elite responses are not significantly shaped by formally structured organizations of the poor. Whatever influence lower-class groups occasionally exert in American politics does not result from organization, but from mass protest and the disruptive consequences of protest.[13]

Piven and Cloward arrived at that stark, controversial, some might say outrageously wrong conclusion by a careful review of studies by historians, political scientists, sociologists, and government policy analysts. The footnotes to each page and the extensive bibliography at the end of their book testify to a long, careful job of historical political sociology. The scope is tremendous in comparison with the previous kinds of studies, so of course the degree to which their analysis constitutes proof of their thesis will be argued for years. In other words, answers bring further questions. It is in just such a way that our knowledge of society advances.

In general, all four kinds of studies on the nature and effects of citizen participation challenge the conventional wisdom. In this case, it is the "wisdom" that participating can count for much at present in American society, regardless of whether or not one has power as a result of one's position in the economy. And to the extent that we accept what the studies say, were are forced to ask further questions, questions both for research and for eventual political action. For example, why does voting seem to have so little effect? Why have government programs for citizen participation been set up to neutralize any real power by citizens? Why must the poor turn to disruption and violence to get anywhere? In this way social research has an inevitably destructive effect on the status quo, on the myths that keep the present society intact.

A knowledge of the sociology of politics is a necessary first step in changing the nature of these politics, a requirement for an educated citizenry, a substitute for a nation of sheep. It is especially important to look at the power structures at the community level, structures citizens are trying to affect and change. For most of us, the community is the largest political arena for our meaningful action. It is to this field of action that we now turn.

Community Power Structure

Let's begin with a definition of *power*. One of the oldest and sturdiest is that it is the ability of one individual or group (A) to make another individual or group (B) do what A wants them to do, whether B wants to or not. In most cases power is a mixture of *authority*, belief on B's part that it is legitimately right for A to demand that B do what A wants and *force*, A's possession of the means of violence to compel B under the threat of harm or depriving B of his resources. A *power structure* is a specific arrangment of individuals and groups that can be characterized as having a power center and a top-to-bottom structure, with the decision makers and order givers at the center or top and the order takers and passive accepters of decisions at the periphery or at the bottom. Very few power relationships and power structures can be permanently maintained with the force component alone. You can't keep a cop on every corner and raw force will eventually compel armed revolt. But *some* force stands behind every social order. To look at a community and not ask the basic questons about power is to be impossibly naive. It is also incompetent if you are doing a sociological investigation of the community.

Let's start with what appears to be a simple question but isn't: Who runs this town? In order to answer a question like that, sociologists have devised various research strategies and have developed models of the power structure of a community—diagrams illustrating the outlines of power relations. Part of the debate in this area of sociology is caused by different *assumptions* about how the research ought to be done, and how the decision making process works from day to day in any given community. Historically, sociologists began with simple models in small, relatively uncomplicated communities. As time passed, more social scientists, including close cousins in political science, got into the act and studied more complex and larger areas. We can briefly review some models here to give you a sense of the ways that the original questions about communities raised by Park were elaborated on and revised, and used to study the political world of community activity.

A town they called "Middletown" was one of many small communities studied by the husband-wife team of Robert and Helen Lynd. In their book *Middletown* and their followup *Middletown in Transition* they view the power structure as a simple pyramid:

At the top was a family far more wealthy than most. It owned the factory where most people worked, and was in a controlling position over the town bank and the formal political system of the community.[14] In a small town in the South with a giant cotton mill, the mill owner would occupy this position. In a larger city than that studied by the Lynds, Floyd Hunter found a slightly more complicated version of the pyramid. The official power structure, the elected politicians, appeared out front and publicly carried out decisions already made by the true power structure, the banks and large corporations of the city.[15] The picture looked like this, according to Hunter:

This kind of simple model making created a controversy, and a series of studies were done to critique the model. These described a more complicated process at work. One that became a classic was Robert Dahl's book about New Haven, *Who Governs?*[16] He chose the title carefully because he intended to prove that there wasn't just *one* elite running New Haven. Rather, he contended, there were a series of elites, each representing a "world," each having its power figures. The groups together made things happen in the city. No one group could act alone:

In this kind of a setup, a good organizer, such as Mayor Lee of New Haven, could get the different elites to work together. But critics of Dahl's work noted that in many of the cases he discussed, the real power was in the first triangle—the big-business one, which also included the financial powers in town. The critics noted further that the leaders of big business were also often leaders at Yale (on university boards) and were members of the New Haven social elite. Really, they said, Dahl's model should look like this:

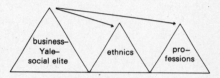

Or, as the English social critic George Orwell said, all of the animals are equal, but some are more equal than others.[17] If the business-society-university combine was against something, it didn't happen. On issues of lesser importance, not affecting the whole city, the relevant elite would decide by itself.

But what about really big cities? Edward Banfield and Roberts Wilson studied Boston, San Francisco, and Jersey City, and they found a complex situation. So did another study, Raymond Vernon's book on New York City.[18] The complex areas of responsibility, the warring ethnic and racial groups, and the increasing financial and political importance of the state and *federal* governments meant that power did not automatically reside in any one place. A skilled operator could use his place in the structure as a location from which to give favors to others to build up a system of obligations and then call on them. Some such figures—Mayor Daley of Chicago, for example—have been elected officials who used a political machine to become a power broker.[19] Others have been able to build a power empire on a strategic resource. The best example here is Robert Moses, the great road and bridge builder of New York City and Long Island. Moses parlayed dollars gained from tolls from the Triboro Bridge into a political empire, the New York Port Authority. Robert Caro, in *The Power Broker*, explains:

Even had the records been available, of course, the public might not have understood their significance. For Moses was a political boss with a difference. He was not the stereotype with which Americans were familiar. His constituency was not the public but some of the most powerful men in the city and state, and he kept these men in line by doling out to them, as Tammany ward bosses once handed out turkeys to the poor at Thanksgiving, the goodies in which such men were interested, the sugar plums of public relations retainers, insurance commissions and legal fees. This man, personally honest in matters of money, became the locus of corruption in New York City. Robert Moses made himself the ward boss of the inner circle, the bankroller of the Four Hundred of politics. Far from being above the seamier aspects of politics, he was—for decades—the central figure about whom revolved much of the back-stage maneuvering of New York City politics. Triboro's public relations retainers ran to a quarter of a million dollars a year, its legal fees to a quarter million, its insurance commissions to half a million—a total of a million dollars a year. Moses parcelled out retainers, fees and commissions to city and state political leaders on the basis of a very exact appraisal of their place in the political pecking order.[20]

Some confusion is created by this kind of community study we have been considering because each one uses a slightly different method to determine who has the power. Some, such as Hunter's, ask people to rank a list of names, chosen in turn from lists of the "influential" people in town. But do the most respected have the most power? Other studies assume that true power ultimately rests only with the wealthy, the owners of the banks and the biggest businesses in a town. Then they watch how they operate. Yet community action programs have sometimes won against the combined power of city bosses and disinterested, perhaps even racist banks. We sociologists need to do a series of community studies that all use the *same* techniques for studying community power structure, and to do the series on towns and cities of different size and complexity. We also need to agree ahead of time just what we will use as a definition of power. The debate, and interest, lies at least in part in the fact that this is still a new, exciting, and rapidly developing field in community studies. For students of society and for community residents too, the results can make a real difference, if change in the community is a topic on the agenda.

A limitation of all such studies, however, is their focus on a town or city. Power is increasingly *national* in our society. It is located in one giant headquarters, in New York City, and also in Washington,

D.C. lobbying offices of these corporations. With every passing decade it is becoming increasingly impossible to understand power structures and decision-making processes unless this is taken into account. For example, Vidich and Bensman's study of an upstate New York town found that large corporations from elsewhere bought up locally owned companies and turned them into branches. The far-away companies could now make decisions that would make their little town thrive or die without the older town power structure having a say.

Many political scientists have pointed out that with the passage of time, power is becoming centralized in a smaller and smaller number of banks and corporations, which in turn are working more and more closely with government to make decisions affecting all our lives. As of 1979, less than three percent of all U.S. industrial firms owned over 80 percent of all industrial assets. There is a debate, however, on the significance of this centralization of power. It is to this issue that we now turn.

Corporate Power: A Debate Between Two Theories

Each step up a mountain trail widens the view you can see over your shoulder. With each step, we have been widening our sociological view. When studying "life in the small" the sociology of political life is concerned with the complex mysteries between people, in the area of power. Widening the view to citizen participation, and then to community power structure, added yet another level of complexity. With complexity of topic comes disagreement over what it is and how to analyze it. Thus it should come as no surprise that sociologists disagree about what's in this big picture and especially about the issue of corporate power in a democratic society. Is it really true that the 500 largest corporations run our society, that voting is a sham, a put-up job staged to get us to think we are affecting decisions that have already been made behind closed doors? If it is, how do you *prove* that it is? If not, what is the evidence against it? And just what is meant here by *running* our society, anyway? Note the definition problems, the research problems, the even more basic problem of framing the question. The use of a theory—a systematic way of framing questions and of relating questions to one another in such a way that they can be tested as a whole—is handy at this point.

A historical review of the way sociologists have approached this problem of using theory could easily take a whole volume. But a brief sketch may help to get this issue into perspective. The first great sociological theorists were much impressed with the impact industry was having on society as it grew and began to flourish in the mid-1800s. Marx early spotted the power that the new industrialists would have. He saw their leverage as the owners of the new machines that would make the wealth and as the employers of more and more people. Max Weber observed that the growth of industry meant the ultimate bureaucratizing of the world, the creation of rigidity in human relations. Auguste Comte was a little more optimistic. He felt that the system was inevitably coming and that sociologists would and should work within it. He had been an engineering student—optimistic about industry like many engineers—and had come to believe that the new power figures could be convinced to be concerned with the welfare of their workers and the general good of the society they were helping to build.

Those who followed Marx and his theory took a different view of what was happening. They did not blame particular factory owners or think the solution lay with reforming them. The problem was more basic, they thought. It was the whole setup. In order to make a profit the owners had to put money in their pockets that really the workers on the assembly line had made for them. There was a *conflict of interest* between these two groups, the industrial capitalists and the factory-based working class. What one gained the other lost. The only way out of this situation was to change its very nature. There should be one class; the people who owned the place should be the same group as the ones working in it.

But how to get there? In Russia, the first nation that had a socialist revolution, in 1917, a new political party seized control of the factories and established what Lenin, their master theorist, called "the dictatorship of the proletariat."[21] And he *did* mean dictatorship. Claiming inspiration from Marx, and acting at the point of a gun, the new revolutionary government took land away from the great landowners and peasants and developed new public industry. Lenin and his co-workers built their state bureaucracy on the firm foundation of the old state bureaucracy of the czars of Russia, putting their own men in at the top. Gradually a new form of society evolved. In it the state was all-powerful. The people had very little in the way of civil rights; they had especially little freedom to criticize the operations of the state supposedly acting in their interests and in their name. On the other hand, there was no more starvation, of which there had been a lot under czars, and education was now universally available. So was health care. Doctors had to go to work in a new socialized-medicine program or leave the country. And as with China years later, for most of the people, the millions of the starving and hope-less, no matter how much dictatorship eventually resulted, this revolution was still exchanging nothing for something. The problem with Lenin's use of Marx, and the state he created, was that he adopted Marx's ideas in a direction Marx would not have wanted to go. Also Marx analyzed *capitalism;* Russia had little or none to analyze in those days.

In the West, capitalism has gone through stages, from that of the nineteenth century robber baron or cowboy capitalism state to that of the modern super-sophisticated corporation, working closely with the government at local, state, and federal levels. Does the nineteenth century situation of small governments and isolated, competing capi-talist firms still exist in the West? Is Marx's original theory still relevant without modification, to *either* the modern Soviet Union or the modern America? Just what kind of theory can be used to grasp today's complicated power relations between citizens, the corpora-tions, and the state?

Many theories deal with these issues, but two in wide use today are especially helpful—and in competition with each other as "the" way of looking at the present field of forces and predicting the future. They are generally called the *pluralist model* and the *modern Marxian model.* [22] The *pluralist* model, doing for the nation what Dahl did for New Haven, views America as a collection of interest groups, of competing elites, each organized and fighting to get what it wants by influencing the government through the political process. The gov-ernment itself is viewed by pluralists as neutral, and no elite or combination of elites is seen to systematically win out in the long run. This model makes no assumptions about the basic long-term direction and development of a society. It is a narrowly political model that does not directly use such factors as technological change and economic ownership as main explaining factors. Using the model requires looking in great detail at the groups involved, what each is struggling for, and who is getting what. Alliances and allegiances are plotted and analyzed. The process of political infighting—for example, in the halls of Congress—is described in detail. Who wins and loses each battle is explained in a model that assumes that all the actors are *potentially* able to win sometimes. It is assumed that the government is a neutral kind of battleground, or a neutral party that has to be won over to the side of, for example, consumers or oil companies.

Most newspaper analysis, and most of the studies of the Ralph Nader researchers, use this kind of model. The idea that the entire game could be stacked from the start is not considered. Yet many studies document almost a half century of steady wins by the corporations against worker and consumer interests, with a slight and rather marginal victory from time to time.[23]

The *modern Marxian* model makes a different set of assumptions about two of the key actors in national political battles, the corporations and the state. In all of Marxian theory, since the original work of Marx and Engels, the owners of the corporations—the means of producing goods—are called the capitalist class. Each other class is defined and explained in terms of its basic economic self-interest and the political action it takes (or doesn't take) to protect that interest. Class struggle—especially between capitalists and the employee class —is a continual process. Modern Marxian theory has developed since the time of Marx in ways that fit more closely the complex realities of today, in the West. It is more realistic than some early Marxian work in noticing the splits and fights between different industries— capitalists do not act as a uniform bloc. But in the long run the class does get together to protect itself when its interests are threatened.

A second major actor in the modern version of this theory is the state. Modern Marxians define the state as all the branches of government, including all the regulatory agencies. The modern version of the theory has updated the original ideas of Marx on the basis of changes in the real arrangements since his time, in relations between capitalists and the state. When Marx wrote, it seemed to him that the state simply did what the corporate capitalist class said it should do. Today the situation is a lot more subtle, according to the modern theory. In its role as the preserver of "the health of the economy," the United States government and its agencies make decisions, especially in the area of economic policy, that are intended to keep the train on its tracks. But that train is a *capitalist* train, running on capitalist tracks, and that's the rub. So, according to this theory, it is not an accident that, for instance, presidential economic advisers recommend that the price of gasoline should be raised to prevent us from buying too much of it (when we need it to go to work) rather than rationing it, which would cut into profits for the oil industry.

What is especially important here is the modern Marxian understanding of the limits that are put on the state's freedom of action. Take Ralph Nader-style consumer action. When consumer groups start to make minor gains against the auto industry, for example, the government has to pull back at a certain point and refuse to give in to these groups. That point is the point at which the auto industry says it is "endangered." And what does "endangered" mean? *Profits* are endangered, say the auto makers, and "that means we'll have to fire workers." In this way, the theory shows why the state in a capitalist society *must* work in the long run not neutrally, as some kind of referee, but rather in the long run to preserve the power and profits of the capitalist class, and especially those of the largest 500 corporations and the largest 15 banks.[24]

This analysis also includes an explanation for the fact that an arm of the state (a particular regulatory agency, for example) will occasionally make trouble for a particular corporation in a particular sector of the economy. For example, although the Occupational Health and Safety Administration (OSHA) is usually sympathetic to the problems of business in paying for safety equipment to protect workers, a few years ago the plastics industry was hit by the OSHA staff for letting workers get cancer and die from polyvinyl chloride poisoning. Worker-health activists and unions pushed, and then the feds acted. Precisely, say the Marxian analysts—an occasional act by the state like this deflects people's attention for the long-run, low-profile business as usual behavior of the federal government in this area, like many others, when it refuses to press the *majority* of corporations on the *majority* of issues which might affect their profits in a significant way.

Note the research problem these competing theoretical explanations pose about the real function of the state in an advanced capitalist economy such as the United States. In the present context, Marxians would contend that it's not simply a matter of assessing how much power the activists do or don't have in a particular fight. That is a good first step, and is about as far as pluralist analysis goes, aft er the step has been taken for each group active in the situation. It's more a matter of using the theroy to assess what the results *mean.* Guided by a pluralist model, the research might focus down on a given year, a given corporation, and one or a series of fights on one issue. If the activitsts win, well, that shows that pluralism is at work, say the pluralist theorists. But what if the activist groups were pushing on the polyvinyl chloride case and the OSHA bureaucracy had been under attack to do something to show it wasn't always a captive of industry? The pluralist theorist would say, "Aha, my case is proved."

But so would the Marxian—in a longer-term perspective and with a broader view, especially on the non-neutral role of the state. OSHA, from a Marxian viewpoint, was at least in part a public relations agency, not a real enforcer of worker safety. Marxists and pluralists would disagree as to *why* changes were occuring, and what the consequences of changes will be. So the debate goes on, and it stimulates further research. It is in part a debate over the assumptions behind the theory, and in part a debate about the scope of the analysis. It is also a debate over the time frame during which research should be carried on, especially about the need to use a long-term historical perspective. Each camp learns from the other, however. We are now beginning to get pluralist analyses that are historical and Marxian analyses that go into detail that was always the strong point of the pluralist approach.

Early Marxian analyses sometimes tended toward oversimplification and some namecalling. But a new generation of careful Marxian scholars are working, especially in history, economics, and sociology. They have updated the older version of Marxian theory, and are developing a new body of genuinely scholarly articles and books that challenge the pluralist appproach. All this makes for a much more interesting field for professors and for students too. Argument, challenge, counterargument, always with evidence, is a sign that a field in academia is alive. I'm pleased to report that even in the quiet of recent years this debate, over who runs America, is alive and well.

The Fight for Pleasant Valley—Round Two

It takes time to write a book and time to revise it. In the space of time between the first and final draft of this book, a whole extra year passed—a year since the events in Pleasant Valley reported in the last chapter. The issues were different in this final year—they were political in the large sense of the term. Discussing them here will give you some sense of how the concepts of political socialization, citizen participation, power, and power struture apply to a particular political struggle, in this case ours in the valley.

As we reported earlier, we had tried for three years to change the attitudes of the people of Batesville about the desirability of destroying the valley. Much time during the last year was spent speaking to people on corners, appearing at local town clubs (Rotary, Lions), and conversing with the small shopkeepers on Main Street. We decided that the message of "ecology" simply would not sell in Batesville, but community pride (not wanting to be known as Dumptown, U.S.A.) and community concern with jobs and local economy (dumps are bad for business) could be sold as values, because they were close enough to those of the majority of the community yet were at the same time a way of communicating about the impact of the dump on the community as a whole.

Our second strategy was, whenever possible, to have the message be conveyed to townspeople by those who were friends of our cause but who did *not* live in the valley. That way, we could identify our cause as an all-Batesville one and not simply as "the Pleasant Valley gang's fight," as one story described it. We began to make headway. But we also began to run out of money and some steam—at least the original people in the valley did. You can have only so many yard sales.

The critical events of the past year have revolved around the issue of the wider power structure of the society around Batesville, particularly the state government, with its need to find a location for a big dump for the garbage it no longer allows in smaller town dumps, which have been closed one by one. In all, the latest phase definitely shows Batesville as a small town in a mass society.

A low point was reached about five months after the end of last chapter's news. Several cases we brought into court, suing local town boards for breaking their own laws, were lost on appeal to higher state courts. Suddenly the town was faced with the reality of another thirty-five-acres of garbage and trash, the first entering wedge of the big dump. Community action of direct sort arose at this point. We got enough support from the rest of town to march, almost 300 strong, on Town Hall to protest, with garbage cans banging, trash strewn in the street by children, banners waving, and someone else (not me) riding that horse. The people chanted, "Dump the dump! Dump the dump!" That same slogan was on a bumper sticker we had printed up and used at fairs to raise money for the legal fight. The rumor mill was cranked up for others, but most of what they were saying didn't seem too far off base. People were afraid the whole town would eventually become a dump, with the valley only the first step. The businessmen began to fear that Batesville might never catch up to the nearby towns. The political socialization of Batesville was now well under way. Finally, for the first time in three years, a town board said no about the permission to use the land in the valley, the thirty-five-acre plot. The Cleanliness Corporation will appeal that, of course.

The federal government also began to enter the picture at this point. The U.S. Securities and Exchange Commission had been investigating the Cleanliness Corporation about the possibility of illegal practices having to do with company operations. Apparently the 150 acres in the valley that the company had bought had first been bought by a former officer of the company privately and then sold at an overinflated price to the company itself. The SEC was involved because the compnay was on the stock exchange and stockholder profits were affected by such kinds of dealings. At the same time, other federal agencies began to put out reports on the dangers of landfills to health and safety and the environment—methane gas explosions, pollution—all very real to us and specially relevant to a dump planned to be uphill from a river that millions of dollars of federal money had already been spent on, to clean it up. Our Congressman, Michael Harrington of Massachusetts, a sponsor of the river cleanup and an environmentalist, wrote a strong letter to the governor and the state environment people, supporting our stand.

This last Fall before the book went to press brought even more changes. First, our Congressman decided not to run again. Second, the politics at the state level changed, probably not in our favor. Again note the increasing importance of the out-of-community factors. During this last period the pros and cons look this way. First, our town voted in November 1978, in a nonbinding referendum, against the dump, by a 3-to-1 margin. Also an antidump local politician was elected as our state representative to the legislature.

But none of the myriad local town officials who have been pro-dump all along have yet been turned out of office, because very few people could be convinced to oppose them politically by running for local office. Even more to the point, the resources of the Cleanliness Corporation for legal aid are extensive, unlike the town's. Even more important than that, a new pro-business and anti-environmentalist governor is in office in Massachusetts, and the old environment people at the top have resigned or have been fired. There is every expectation that environmental protection will not be as strictly enforced by the new governor. While some regional planning agencies warn about what might happen to the river, the new state government still has the problem of what to do with the trash. And the town of Batesville was one of the few to vote against the new governor. It is a basically Democratic town that voted for the Republican candidate.

Thus, in a real political battle, *all* the issues we have reviewed in this chapter come into play: political socialization (and changing it), citizen participation (making it happen and count), the community power structure, and the wider power structure, especially the role of the state and the corporations. It turned out that the perceived power structure of the town (perceived by us, that is) turned out not to be as monolithic as we feared. It also turned out that we *could* socialize people politically. But the town apathy remains a key factor, as to the economic interests of the Cleanliness Corporation and the state—very powerful when ranged against this small town. But the town vote is 3 to 1 against now, and another year has passed with no dump. The longer we fight, the more the state thinks of alternate sites for the dump, and the more money we cost the Cleanliness Corporation. One step at a time!

From Study to Action

The world is full of people who are spectators of, but not participants in, the events that shape their lives. Sociology is a tool for understanding the setting within which great events and small occur. And sociology can give information for political action. *But it cannot act for you, nor can it guarantee that your action will be successful.* This is important to say here because study can become not simply a preparation for action, but rather a substitute for it.

Most of the world looks with a mixture of puzzlement and scorn at typical American attitudes toward social action and social change. To be active about some social problem for a year or two, and then forget it if success is not apparent, is a widespread phenomenon here. If the noise and theatrics of the Sixties didn't work, give up while the power structure and the capitalist class works out what I call "the big squeeze"—the rise in the cost of everything without a similar rise in our wages, a tremendous rise in profits for large corporations while ordinary people fall farther and farther behind. Also the Seventies were passive because the analysis was spotty, the connections not made. But the future need not be a repetition of the past. What will be necessary to prevent that is a refusal of knee-jerk reactions to situations, or of mass media analysis of them, and a willingness to sit down with others and think about what can be done now and what over the next five years. It will require the ability to think sociologically. But this whole book has been about that—developing that skill for yourself, starting to look at the world as a sociologist might.

For Further Reading

Walter Ullmann. *Individual and Society in the Middle Ages.* Baltimore: Johns Hopkins University Press, 1956.
   A short, brilliant summary of the conflicting points of view held by differ-ent social strata in the Middle Ages. Rule from the top down—and the power of the church over men's minds—is contrasted with the slow growth of local home rule and the idea of citizen rights and democracy, over five centuries.
C. Wright Mills. *The Power Elite.* New York: Oxford University Press, 1956.
   Mills' book was considered radical when it first came out, but now simply seems thorough and scholarly. It remains a well-documented, classic anal-ysis of the power of the military-industrial complex within American politics. This work influenced a whole younger generation of American sociologists.
Frances Fox Piven and Richard Cloward. *Poor People's Movements: How They Succeed, Why They Fail.* New York: Basic Books, 1977.
   The civil rights movement, union movement, and welfare rights move-ment are analyzed to help understand the power, and the powerlessness, of poor and working class Americans over the last half century. An excel-lent description of the hurly-burly of politics. They controversially sug-

gest that only the threat of violence or actual violence as a form of protest will get the poor what they want.

George Orwell. *Animal Farm.*

George Orwell. *1984.*

Two classic fables or fantasies by the great English social critic of totalitarianism. Especially good on the issue of bureaucracy in the service dictatorship, and on thought control; he was criticizing the Soviet Union in much that he wrote. Excellent on the difference between official ideology and true experience by ordinary people.

Robert A. Caro. *The Power Broker. Robert Moses and the Fall of New York.* New York: Knopf, 1974.

This huge (more than 1000 pages) biography matches its huge subject— the way Robert Moses built a political empire and planned the shape of modern New York City. Not at all boring in spite of its length, it gives you the feel for a how a master builder and wheeler-dealer built a personal power structure stronger than the city or the state.

Niccolo Machiavelli. *The Prince.*

This short, and classic, introduction to the role of the man of power has now been in print for four hundred years, and is as relevant today as then. In one of the first objective analyses of what works if you wish to stay in power, Machiavelli laid out a series of short principles on what to do and not do.

Carole Pateman. *Participation and Democratic Theory.* Cambridge, England: Cambridge University Press, 1970.

A scholarly and comprehensive critical review of all of the ideas and issues grouped under the topic "citizen participation." Participation in decision-making is contrasted for capitalist and socialist societies. Special attention is paid to planning and work as occasions for participation.

Ralph Miliband. *The State in Capitalist Society.* New York: Basic, 1969.

Ralph Miliband. *Marxism and Politics.* New York: Oxford University Press, 1977.

Two modern discussions of power, economics and social change by a leading modern Marxian political scientist. The first looks at the issue of the degree to which the state cannot be neutral within a capitalist economy, and the role of the mass media in such cases. The second shows the strengths, and the weaknesses, of Marxian theory in dealing with political phenomena, as well as explaining how and why the theory "died" as a true research tool in Eastern Europe.

Chapter

SIX

Thinking Sociologically

Teachers vary. Some are inspired and can lead you into thoughts you might never have had. Others, alas, are not so inspired, or are just putting in their time. A teacher may mumble, or it may be your luck to get one during the term his or her marriage is breaking up, and other things on the mind may get in the way of teaching. The luck of the draw is also an issue with books on sociology, especially textbooks. You didn't choose the text, but you will be reading it. Some are better than others. And in any case, and also in spite of this little book of mine, you may still find yourself wondering whether sociology is necessary at all.

What *is* this field called sociology? In part it is its subject matter, the things it looks at. Each of the previous chapters was about one of these main areas of sociology—a taste of how sociologists approach those great slices of experience out of which your life and mine are built. But most basically a field is not its subject matter. Rather, a field is a way of looking at and thinking about that subject matter. For example, throughout the Middle Ages magicians and alchemists toyed with the chemicals and organic material in their laboratories. But this wasn't chemistry. Chemistry began with a theory of the elements, an attitude toward the material, and a model—Mendeleev's periodic table of the elements. As with chemistry, so with sociology. It's a way of looking, and a way of thinking. But in sociology the range of ways of looking is far wider than in the natural sciences, and the reasons for looking also vary far more. Some sociologists think of their goal as understanding in the humane or the artistic sense; others have the goal of prediction as in physics.

In spite of this diversity, which I have tried to illustrate by showing the different approaches sociologists use and some debates they have, there are some attitudes and aims they all share. First, there are a series of ways of looking and thinking that are shared by all the social sciences but are particularly prominent in sociology. These I call separating out the general from the particular, taking a detached point of view, having a sense of process, challenging conventional wisdom, and taking an interest in alternatives. Each is a central element in thinking sociologically. Then there is the most basic strategy of all—asking the uniquely *sociological* question.

The General from the Particular

Sociologists share one aim with all those involved in scientific work. They seek to derive general principles from a series of specific incidents. How this is done will depend on which sociologist is doing it, and the type of research approach. For example, here is Robert Merton writing about a way of developing a more specific test of Durkheim's theory of anomie, or a breakdown in shared values, in order to apply the theory to other phenomena besides suicide. He notes the need for a theory, to serve his purposes, midway between great abstractions of a Marx or a Durkheim and the descriptions of events found in the daily newspaper, which works in a *ad hoc,* or simple and immediate, fashion:

> By this time, it was bound to become evident that the notion of anomie had very broad implications that went far beyond the special phenomenon of suicide, just as it was evident that the concept was not an *ad hoc* idea, unconnected with ways of thinking about social and cultural structure. Obviously, the immediate theoretical problem was to find a way of construing *systematically,* rather than in *ad hoc* descriptive fashion, the types of behavioral responses to anomie. As is evident now, but was not evident then, this required a theoretical construction of the middle range.[1]

Merton was trying to categorize the ways in which people deviated from social norms and broad-scale underlying social values, and the form of action the deviation took. He came up with the idea of the "opportunity structure"—the extent to which a person or group can get what the society says is desirable to want while still using the society's normal way of getting there. Getting rich by going to college and law school or by pushing dope depends on where you start out:

> . . . the theory turned on the notion of opportunity-structure: the location of people in the social structure that affected the probability of their moving toward culturally emphasized goals in ways that were normatively approved.[2]

Survey researchers are more likely to work with a limited set of clearly spelled out hypotheses. Rules for decisions on accepting or rejecting the hypotheses are set out ahead of time, and questions deal with very precise topics. Think, for example, of the voting surveys we reviewed in the last chapter. By comparision, how does Merton know that his theory has been proved? Or is that the complete aim? In fact, Merton and the voting researchers are not doing precisely the same thing using different techniques. In Merton's case (though some in his camp in sociology might vehemently disagree) there is as much art as science in whatever gets abstracted out and called a theory.

The relation between theory and research has been much discussed, and importantly by Merton himself. He was interested in the problem, and he worked closely with a large survey-research bureau at Columbia University, the Bureau of Social Research. There many of his graduate students and some Ph.D.s were involved in trying out his middle-range theories on a wide range of social phenomena. Over lunch they would feed the results back to him. He did the theory, they did the research, and they talked with one another. The combination of theory and research has far greater payoffs than just newspaper description, because with a theory you can see connections to other things that without the theory would seem just unrelated.

Most importantly, generalizing involves the problem of scope. There is always a trade-off—knowing some things well in detail but not much of the big picture, or describing the big picture but not being terribly sure of the details. Some sociologists specialize in one topic, others are more interested in the big picture and the historical long run. In my opinion, both kinds of sociologists are necessary and each can learn from the other.

So where are we? How can you or I be sure that the sociologist has indeed gotten it straight, generalized the right conclusion out of the buzzing confusion around him or her? There is no way. Coming upon the data, a second sociologist and then a third may disagree and come to different conclusions. Yet this is not basically different from the problem chemists have. All science progresses by disagreements about conclusions from the data. Its just that the room for disagreement is very large in sociology because of the complexity of the subject matter.

Disagreements in sociology are large also for another very special reason. What the sociologist observes is a fellow creature whose privacy can never be really penetrated by the techniques of sociology. Furthermore, that subject can probably read, and may read the reports of the sociologist and agree or disagree with them. When was the last time an atom observed another atom? When was the last time a molecule acted differently in response to the drama critic's reviews? In a word, sociology reflects back on itself, for it causes changes in the social world itself, including the perception of its own findings. If there weren't enough room for argument, just on the issue of accuracy and correct conclusions, there is *that* to guarantee a complicated life for sociology. Yet, in spite of it, sociology makes the effort. A medal for bravery might be in order, if nothing else. Or is it simply that fools rush in where angels fear to tread?

A Detached Point of View

This essential characteristic of sociological thinking is not what it may seem to be. "Detached" here does not mean uncaring or disinterested. You might find a sociologist or two who fit that description, but most sociologists care a lot about society and are likely to have opinions, both public and private, about what ought to be done about it. To be detached when attempting to look at the world from the sociological point of view demands something more difficult, personally, than to be uncaring. It demands a willingness to wipe slates clean, to admit that previous attitudes toward a group, toward a trend, or even toward yourself might have been the product of a particular set of social circumstances. You won't find it easy to get distance from your own prejudices—what you "know" is so and "has always been so" about some group of people or some political arrangement in the nation. Worst of all, you may kid yourself into thinking that you have become completely neutral about yourself and your present position in society, and your views on the present social order. You aren't—that I can guarantee.

Becoming "detached" is not a permanent state—sociologists are not bloodless, expressionless creatures. If an occasional one may put this image across in the classroom, try them at the party at the regional sociology meetings, or at the supermarket. One becomes detached during the act of analysis only—and only for the analysis, not as some kind of personality change. After the analysis, action is and in many cases ought to be not only possible, but also desirable. No, detached here has the special meaning of not letting previous prejudices, hunches, even strong wishes about the way you hope findings will come out affect the way you treat the data.

Max Weber agonized about this problem. He began by noting that what you choose to study gives away your idea of what is important (and by implication unimportant) to you. Then, he observed, comes the hard part. *All* the evidence on a problem must be marshaled, no matter how much of a mess this makes of your original hunch about the true cause or the probable outcome of some social process you have been studying. This gets hard to do for a number of reasons. First, in choosing a research strategy—the *way* of doing research— we may stress one part of a problem and deemphasize another, the part that might weaken or reverse the results. This is a form of bias, especially if the experienced researcher knows in a secret personal way that it is being done. Second, we are fallible creatures when it comes to recording data. How very easy it is to ignore what we don't want to see, and thus how very important it becomes to fight against this.

What holds for gathering and recording information holds even more for analyzing it. There are some kinds of research operations where one group of researchers gather the raw data and a second group interpret it under the observation of a third, senior group. Research consulting firms often operate this way. This may not guarantee detachment and objectivity. It may instead simply multiply error and bias, as well as generate a kind of disinterest in getting good data by that first group. The danger of the hired-hand research provided by some research consulting firms lies in the boredom of the field hands themselves. *Involved* detachment, then, is the ideal state —caring not about what the results turn out to be, but rather about the purity of the way you get to them.

In this regard what about the leftist Marxian scholars and researchers in sociology—the sociological "New Left" of the Sixties and Seventies? Intense as they seem, they surely can't be detached, can they? It is true that these researchers and scholars are one special case. To begin with, high standards of scholarship and accuracy of data are especially strictly applied by many in this group to their own work, especially because of the controversial nature of the overall viewpoint itself. In the public eye they are often confused with and lumped with pamphleteers, crazies, and noisemakers and may be called such without being given a chance to respond. In addition— and this I am sorry to see—some have developed their own Marxian social science jargon that it as impenetrable and puzzling to those new to the field as is some of the more standard sociological jargon.

With these people and others the canons of evidence must be applied to the data and a theory must be disprovable as well as provable. Conservative, liberal, and Marxist sociologists alike can be separated, into two groups—those who are willing to frame their own questions and do their analyses in such a way that they can be disproved, and those who are unwilling to admit negative evidence. The latter are practicing religion, not sociology; they are deep in a kind of involvement that usually makes good sociology impossible. This does not mean that sociological research cannot be used for political action. In fact, if you did go into battle, which would you rather have, an accurate assessment of the real strength of the enemy or a scouting report from a flunky who told you what he thought you wanted to hear?

A Sense of Process

Life sometimes seems to have the quality of a series of snapshots, but the sociologist looks for patterns, shapes, and social processes, dimensions that unfold over time. This creates a curious feeling when you first read many sociological studies, a feeling that the authors are being a little too general or even worse, *oversimplifying* a complicated reality. This is one of the hardest problems in shifting from the view of sociology as a color sound movie (which it isn't) to the more accurate view of sociology as a discipline that can abstract out from a complicated reality the essentials that lie beneath it.

Are certain types of sociology set up to grasp these social processes better than others? Yes and no. For example, those who do field participant-observation research are constantly plunged into the realities of relations between people. Yet a team of survey researchers —election pollsters, for example—can develop a sense of direction and evolution of human events in their findings as time goes on, especially if they use more than one wave of interviews. Both kinds of researches get involved in the push and pull of events, the clash of social forces, the winning and losing of struggles between people in the community or over the whole economy. Both do sociological analysis that tries to show direction, reveal contenders, assess the factors in the situation that make for tomorrow's outcomes.

How, then, you might ask, does a sociologist differ from a historian? Haven't the scholarly effort of historians over the centuries been aimed at just such a social process? Again, yes and no. What is distinctly sociological is the attempt to get at all the actors and their comprehension of the world they live in. The interest in the counting, in quantitative measures of social forces at work, is a characteristic sociological invention. Interestingly, it is one that the latest generation of historians have adopted to form a new, sociological history. In the beginning, of course, sociology emerged from history—as I noted, Max Weber considered himself at least in part a historian. One of the characteristics of modern social science is just such separation and then convergence again of approaches. Sociology emerged from history, and now history is borrowing back some of the techniques developed in sociology. Fields of knowledge are in process of change themselves.

But the term "a sense of process" has a more general meaning. Sociologists are concerned with the *dynamics* of relationships—what makes them operate, develop, change, end. Identifying these dynamics is not easy, of course. Yet each area of sociology that you study in the future will be much concerned with these dynamics. For instance, what makes a family work over time? In a community the aim is not just to figure out the power structure. It's to show how that power structure behaves over time, how it acts in a series of situations, how it is likely to operate in the future. In general, sociological study should sensitize you to the ways things are going, how they are evolving. There will always be surprises, of course. But a sociological approach can help you understand the rapidly moving forces out there.

A Challenge to Conventional Wisdom

If people really knew what was going on between them, sociology would have far less reason for existence than it does. But much of what people "know," as we have discovered with some of the research examples, is in fact a series of folk statements, a set of comfortable prejudices, a closet full of oversimplifications. Think of the findings on the shock board, where our assumptions about the niceness of people, and their independence, were subjected to a beating. Sociology and sociologists function as a challenge to these stereotyped ways of understanding social reality. But there is a catch. We can't live without some simplifications, or at least most people can't. Sociology thus can be uncomfortable to people.

Let me give you an example. Whenever I teach political sociology we spend quite a bit of time on the problem of just how much power and influence America's giant corporations have. I make sure the students understand that the *structure* of the social situation—including the role of these companies—should not be confused with the personalities of the individuals who head them up. With a series of real-world consumer issues I try to illustrate the real conflicts of interest that arise. What is sad is this—sometimes the bright son or daughter of a high-level corporate executive starts the course parroting the line of the corporation. By the end of the course the student's viewpoint has changed somewhat—not convicned, but at least willing to see more than one side of these issues. Then she goes home, and gets into a real and basic argument that summer with her father. "For *this* I'm spending so much tuition money!" he exclaims. Just in this way—not to supplant one set of stereotypes with another, but to open up as questions what were previously the closed doors of conventional wisdom, is one of the main gifts of sociology.

But again, note that the gift has another kind of price. A high one, at that. You will never see the world the same again. Regardless of how insane sociology can seem at times, how burdened with the wordy jargon of pedants, how full of textbooks, there is a core to it, a challenge, a training in the reinspection of the things that have made your life comfortable as well as the things that have made it uncomfortable. Why eat of the apple from the tree of knowledge? Look what happened to Adam and Eve! Yet we do have curiosity. We are born with it as a very strong motivating force, in fact, according to all the new studies that directly observe small children. We have a natural curiosity about society—the same curiosity that must have driven the great founders of the field to do *their* work, to ask the first great questions about how and why a society is set up the way it is. And if curiosity and the challenging of old assumptions have a price, well, I encourage you to pay it. The irritation you may cause others by your questions and the pain you may experiece as you reexamine your own assumptions will more than be repaid by a deeper, more genuine understanding of the world out there.

An Interest in Alternatives

One of the oldest folk sayings (as well as one of the ugliest if you like animals) is appropriate here: there is more than one way to skin a cat. Along with social anthropology, a sister discipline, sociology has developed a strong sense that there are alternatives in social arrangements. The functions of the family, for example, can be filled in a variety of ways—by two parents, by three-generation groups, by fathers with custody of their children, by communes in New Hampshire or Colorado. What sociology refuses to do, is to say that one of these arrangements is *better.* Different, yes, but better, no—and it matters not what arrangements are more typical of a given time and place. Much of the fascination of the subject to the ones who work at it full time lies precisely in this amazing flexibility in the ways different societies, or different groups of people within our own, can find to set up the arrangements of daily living. As new forms of relationship develop, which they seem to be doing with great rapidity in our present society, sociologists are there documenting them, studying them, reporting them to others. And *not* usually disapproving of what they see, when they go about it.

Not everybody likes this quality, this characteristic of sociology. Especially to those who are the creatures of their own habits, the field tends to appear as a sort of troublemaker. Whatever else it seems to do, the sociological viewpoint does not routinely accept any observed arrangments as the only possible ones or as necessarily preferable to other alternatives. Nor do sociologists necessarily stand on the side of what society calls "respectable." For example, back in the Fifties, when it was a lot rarer to talk about it than now, Howard Becker wrote an article entitled "On Becoming a Marijuana User."[3] Not that Becker describes his own reaction to the drug. But it was clear that he had spent considerable time among the users. He found their activities and reactions interesting sociologically, and he certainly viewed this culture as a legitimate alternative to the "straight" culture of the time.

What is often said about our New England weather—that it is always changing—could also be said about sociological ideas and approaches. There is a genuine sense of alternative ways of attacking problems; there are even changing fashions in doing so. There has been a considerable amount of narrowmindedness in the past. For instance, the research methods textbooks of twenty years ago came down pretty heavily on statistical survey research methods practically to the exclusion of every other approach. But most textbooks in research methods today will introduce a whole series of different research styles, and give each their due.

Asking the Sociological Question

Life sometimes imitates *The Waltons* or some other family TV show, especially if you have children. My daughter's rabbit, Stripes, has black fur with a small collar of white, and white paws. His home is behind the barn, in a boxlike hutch. He escaped one night not too long ago, out the back door of his dwelling. Running paw prints were found in the snow the next morning, followed by the prints of the local dogs. As if things weren't bad enough, my daughter had just finished reading *Watership Down.* I was recruited in the morning after the escape. I asked myself, "If I were a rabbit, where would I hide?" The hole under the cement in front of the barn door was the only place that came to mind. Fortunately, Stripes was of the same opinion, and I was quickly able to reunite our scared pet and our tearful daughter. While this did earn me high marks as a daddy, it was *not* an example of thinking sociologically. Rather, it was me thinking psychologically, rabbit-psychologically at that, and asking a question about the motivaiton of the individual. There was some empathy here, perhaps, but no sociological strategy. There couldn't be. For what was missing here was a *social order* about which to ask a sociological question. Dogs chasing rabbits do not constitute a society.

Another example can provide a contrast—the mass suicides in Guyana by the followers of the Reverend Jim Jones and the People's Temple, in November of 1978. Here some 900 people died. They died in a ghastly acting out of a series of problems first considered sociologically by Emile Durkheim. They died under the leadership of a kind of authority whose power was first considered in depth by another great sociologist, Max Weber. In the Guyana situation we have a crisis that demands a *sociological* set of questions. But much of the discussion in the mass media was psychological in the months after the event. Psychologists and psychiatrists were the experts most frequently asked to appear on the morning and evening news and talk shows on television. As with Stripes, the questions asked of these experts and the answers they gave were overwhelming psychological. Why did *He* (Jones) do It? Why did *each of the others* play along? What got into their heads? The responses, often in psychiatric jargon, included much talk about personal needs. They were in the main unsatisfying.

Many years ago Emile Durkheim proceded quite differently. Rates of suicide—their frequency in a given place at a given time—are a social phenomenon, he said.[4] And they demand a sociological explanation. What are the social processes and the social factors predisposing individuals to suicide? And what are the advantages of belonging to a tightly knit social organization, which restricts as well as rewards behavior? His research showed that many suicides occurred precisely when social bonds were broken and shared feelings and values disappeared. He pointed to higher rates among old people, among Protestants, among the divorced, and among the suddenly rich or suddenly poor. The fear of loneliness and the need for social bonds are built into us, said Durkheim. A society torn apart is painful to those within it, and one escape is suicide as a result of isolation, of anomie, or normlessness. But how do the Guyana victims fit in here? Individual isolation was not their situation. It was the situation they had fled by joining the Temple.

The role of religion and religious groups, said Durkheim, becomes even more important in this modern world where so many changes are taking place and so many are left isolated. The religious group provides a sense of belonging to a community. To join with others can be attractive, and cults tend to be more all-encompassing in their demands and bonds than large, impersonal churches. Many of the Temple members were black, old, divorced, unemployed, or otherwise marginal. The Temple provided the bonds, the belonging, the escape from anomie. But joining a group does not necessarily make you invulnerable to suicide, noted Durkheim. Precisely that union to others might mean that at some time you might be asked to die on their behalf if the union is really strong. That is one of the things wars are to the soldiers who fight in them—at least what they are asked to believe they are. In our own history it was easier for many soldiers to see what they were fighting for in World War II, where the Hitler experience was a clear threat to all, than in Vietnam. But dying for others has meaning only if the individual is truly integrated into the social group. Kamikaze pilots of the Japanese air force in World War II were example of what Durkheim called *altruistic suicides.* They ran their planes into American ships for Japan and the Emperor, and were trained to do so from the start. The People's Temple had a ceremony with similar thinking. The initiation rite into the People's Temple, one repeated at many intervals, was a mock suicide as a group, drinking from an unpoisoned vat of fruit drink. The commitment to the group was symbolized this way. What was bought was an escape from the anomie and loneliness of modern society.

But, you must ask, wasn't Jones crazy? Yes, probably, I would reply, but that has very little to do with the sociological question. The sociological question involves an investigation of the social genesis of the group, its socialization practices, its concept of relationships, career, community, and politics. And only through exploring the sociological question can the mass social act of group sucide be seen as what it was. To begin with, the economic and social pressures on almost all of us these days hit particularly hard on the poor, the black, the old, the divorced, the unemployed including school-dropout adolescents. The poor and helpless turn to the state for support only to find that just when their need is greatest, state services and supports are being cut back. Jones provided an alternative, utopian life style with both economic and social supports and those *restrictions* that Durkheim noted were of particular need to many people. The rites of entry—the mock suicide and the instructions on how to commit suicide—were a test of commitment, a *socialization process,* and a means of subjugating individual will to group needs and then in turn to those of "Dad," Reverend Jones himself. While still in the San Francisco area Jones sent some younger Temple members to local junior colleges, but they were under strict orders not to talk to non-Temple youth. Precisely—the Temple wished to define itself as the normal and the outsiders as the deviants. Too much contact by the youth could lead Temple youth to buy the wider society's definitions of who were the conformists and who the deviant. This might create just the conflict about values that could destroy Temple unity and so destroy the Temple itself.

So, inevitably, they moved. They moved to Guyana to the uncharted jungle, a new world with no competing definitions of the situation. They moved for reasons sociologically not much different from those that motivated the Pilgrims and the other Puritans both to leave England and Holland and come to Massachusetts Bay to set up a "City on a Hill," a utopian community in the wilderness not subject to the poisons of decandent Europe.

But Jones was no John Winthrop (the great Puritan leader), and his cult soon deviated from the Judaeo-Christian tradition it appeared to have at first. In Max Weber's terms, the people who joined were a setup for charismatic leadership, especially one with traditional overtones.[5] Many of the black had come from a tradition of ecstatic, all-encompassing religion in the deep South or the ghetto North, in which the charismatic preacher was very central. Second, the laws of the wider society seemed distant and meaningless to those who were poor and often harassed by state agencies, and Jones offered a different legitimacy and a different source of meaning. He embodied a powerful mixture of charismatic and traditional leadership; the role of preacher is loaded with tradition. This was buttressed by rational-legal sources of legitimacy—letters from public officials he had collected as part of an earlier life in San Francisco politics, in helping deliver the vote of his parishioners, and in service on the city council of San Francisco. Thus Jones used the combination of anomie and his follower's needs for affiliation as well as his legitimacy and took them to Guyana, where the group could only accept the definition of situations from Jones himself. Jones stated again and again that they would be persecuted, that vistors would come and make trouble for them. Finally, a Congressman from the San Francisco area came to the Guyana camp, along with a television camera crew to check up on rumors about the camp which had gotten back to the area from which he and many People's Temple members came from originally. Jones ordered the murder of the Congressman and the camera crew. After this was accomplished, he announced at a general meeting in the Guyana camp that "the time to show unity had come." They were socialized to do what they did, and they killed themselves with, according to the survivors, much group pressure and only a few gunmen on the boundary of the camp. Those who hesitated were shouted down; parents meekly gave the poison to their children before taking it themselves.

Thus what happened in Guyana was not simply individual and group madness. It was a complex event in society. As such it can help show us the necessity of understanding the nature and power of social forces over our lives. We need to know them in order to confront them and decide on our own, as individuals, whether to accept or reject what is offered in our social world. The perspective that the sociological question contributes is one that lets us get outside the prison of our own definitions and fears to see a broader picture of the *alternatives* we have—a view of the forest as well as the trees. Asking the sociological question, therefore, is to look not at the motives of individuals, but to ask questions at which might be called *the social level*—the level of relationships *between* people, their mutual definitions of their social situation, and the ways in which the shared or non-shared group norms and values affect the action of the group and its effect on individuals. Socrates said that the unexamined life was not worth living. Examing yours sociologically might help to prevent its being lived in darkness.

Thinking for Yourself, Sociologically

At the beginning of every new course I make an observation something like this: "My degree of success or failure with you will not be measured by the grades I hand out, or even by the performance you may put on during the course on papers and exams. It will be measured by the use you make in your own life of what you have learned, and by any continuing interest you show—the books you eventually buy on sociology from the local bookstore, later in school and after you graduate, long after this course is over. If you have become interested in thinking sociologically, then the next step will be to make a thorough search with reasonable guides—an instructor and a decent textbook or set of books tied together by a course, of which this book can be the first. You will still have to do most of the work, however. This will include putting up with technical terms, which *are* more abstract than everyday language. It will require learning the precise sociological meanings for terms you already know in a common-sense way, but not as a part of a theory or a model of how a society operates. For those of you used to making black-and-white statements about people, groups, or whole cultures, it will mean learning a thousand shades of gray. It will mean developing new habits of thought about the familiar, the background and foreground of your life. It can mean the disruption of some old relationships, but it can also mean an opening to new ideas and viewpoints.

But perhaps I presume, and exaggerate. Perhaps a course for you is simply one step on the way to a meal ticket, a degree, a degree you need to cash in on a job. I hope not, because sooner or later you may find you have missed a pretty exciting show, the society around you, and your potential place in it. That background to your life could instead become an ever-changing source of fascination, a way of enriching the meaning of your own action and choices while broadening the perspective within which they are made. Sociology can make a difference here. How *much* of a difference depends on you.

Notes

INTRODUCTION: WHY STUDY ANYTHING?

1. Gilbert Highet, *The Immortal Profession: The Joys of Teaching and Learning* (New York: McKay, 1976), p. 1.
2. *Ibid.,* p. 3.
3. Walter Ullmann, *Individual and Society in the Middle Ages* (Baltimore: Johns Hopkins University Press, 1966), pp. 3–50.
4. *Ibid.,* pp. 26–27.
5. Ullmann, pp. 53–98. See also Marc Bloch, *Feudal Society* L. A. Manyon, translator (Chicago: University of Chicago Press, 1968).
6. Karl Marx and Friedrich Engels, "The Communist Manifesto," in Karl Marx and Friedrich Engels, *Basic Writings on Politics and Philosophy,* Lewis Feuer, ed. (Garden City; New York, Doubleday 1959), p. 11.
7. See the wide-ranging and perceptive study by Peter Gay, *The Enlightenment: An Interpretation,* vol I; *The Rise of Modern Paganism,* vol II; *The Science of Freedom* (New York: Simon and Schuster, 1966, 1969).
8. See, for example, Bernard Bailyn, *Ideological Origins of the American Revolution* (Cambridge, Mass.: Harvard University Press. 1967).
9. See Thomas Hobbes, *Leviathan* (New York: Macmillan, 1962).
10. See John Locke, *Of Civil Government* (New York: Gateway Editions, 1960).
11. See Jean-Jacques Rousseau, *Annotated Social Contract,* Charles Sherover, ed. (New York: New American Library, 1974).
12. The key work on this issue, from a historical, psychological, and sociological viewpoint, is Harlan Lane, *The Wild Boy of Aveyron* (Cambridge, Mass.: Harvard University Press, 1977).

13. *Ibid.*, p. 164.

14. Lewis A. Coser, *Masters of Sociological Thought* (New York: Harcourt Brace Jovanovich, 1977), p. 3.

15. An excellent biography of Marx is Isaiah Berlin, *Karl Marx: His Life and Environment* 3rd ed. (New York: Oxford University Press, 1963). For Marx's briefest (and most famous) statement, written with his collaborator Friedrich Engels, see Marx and Engels, *The Communist Manifesto* (New York: Pathfinder Press, 1968).

16. Karl Marx, *The Grundrisse* David McLelland ed. and tr. (New York: Harper and Row, 1972).

17. The demand for sociologists (or economists) to stay neutral in an extremely nonneutral world has led in the past (especially in the early 1900s) to some real problems for those who persisted in speaking out. For an excellent study on this issue, see Mary O. Furner, *Advocacy and Objectivity: The Professionalization of American Social Science* (Lexington: University of Kentucky Press, 1975).

18. How and why Marx's ideas were distorted and modified, and by whom, and yet are still very relevant to today's times is discussed in Ralph Miliband, *Marxism and Politics* (New York: Oxford University Press, 1977).

19. Steven Lukes, *Emile Durkheim: His Life and Work (London: Penguin, 1975), p. 21.*

20. See Furner, *Ibid.*

21. For a more complete discussion see Patricia M. Golden, *The Research Experience* (Boston: Peacock, 1976).

22. Stephen Thernstrom, *Poverty and Progress: Social Mobility in a Nineteenth Century City* (Cambridge, Mass. Harvard University Press, 1964).

23. Erving Goffman, *Asylums* (Chicago: Aldine, 1961).

24. Julius Roth, *Timetables* (Indianapolis, Ind.: Bobbs-Merrill, 1963).

25. A journal called *Qualitative Sociology,* started in 1977, includes examples of sociology through art, including photography.

ONE: DISCOVERING YOURSELF

1. See the discussion by Paul Schilder, *Image and Appearance of the Human Body,* (New York: International Universities Press, 1968).

2. Judy Dunn, *Distress and Comfort* (Cambridge, Mass.: Harvard University Press, 1977), p. 65. See also other volumes in the series *The Developing Child,* published by this press.

3. Roger Brown, *A First Language: The Early Stages* (Cambridge, Mass.: Harvard University Press, 1973).

4. The classic statement of modern ego psychology is Anna Freud, *The Ego and the Mechanisms of Defense* (New York: International Universities Press, 1967).

5. The plea of not guilty by reason of insanity in criminal trials is a continual source of controversy.

6. George Herbert Mead, *George Herbert Mead on Social Psychology*, Anselm Strauss, ed. (Chicago: University of Chicago Press, 1964).

7. Harry Stack Sullivan, *The Interpersonal Theory of Psychiatry*, Helen S. Perry and Mary L. Gawel, eds. (New York: Norton, 1963).

8. Lawrence A. Cremin, *Traditions of American Education* (New York: Basic Books, 1977), p. 123.

9. See the classic article on this subject, Talcott Parsons, "The School Class as a Social System," in Talcott Parsons, *Social Structure and Personality* (New York: Free Press, 1964).

10. See, for example, Robert White, *Ego and Reality in Psychoanalytic Theory* New York: International Universities Press, 1963). On achievement see the study by David McClelland, *The Achievement Motive* (New York: Halsted, 1976).

11. Jonathan Kozol, *Death at an Early Age. The Destruction of the Hearts and Minds of Negro Children in the Boston Public School* (Boston; Houghton Mifflin, 1967, p. 31.

12. For a summary of OEO's action programs for and with the poor, see Sar A. Levitan, *The Great Society's Poor Law* (Baltimore: Jonns Hopkins Press, 1969).

13. Robert Rosenthal and Lenore Jacobson, *Pygmalion in the Classroom: Teacher Expectation and Pupil's Intellectual Development* (New York: Holt, Rinehart and Winston, 1968).

14. Recommended reading here should include the work of Edgar Z. Friedenberg, such as *The Vanishing Adolescent* (Boston: Beacon Press, 1959) and *Coming of Age in America* (New York: Random House, 1965).

15. *High School*, a documentary by Fred Wiseman, is such a film.

16. Erving Goffman, *Stigma. Notes on the Management of Spoiled Identity*. (Englewood Cliffs, N.J.: Prentice Hall, 1963), p. 57.

17. Erving Goffman, *Asylums, Essays on the Social Situation of Patients and Other Inmates*. (Garden City, N.Y.: Doubleday, 1961) p. 143.

18. Erik Erikson, *Childhood and Society*, 2nd ed. (New York: Norton, 1964). pp. 261–262.

19. Erik Erikson, *Young Man Luther* (New York: Norton, 1958). Erik Erikson, *Gandhi's Truth: On the Origins of Militant Nonviolence* (New York: Norton, 1969).

20. Karl Marx, *The Eighteenth Brumaire of Louis Bonaparte* (New York: International Publishers. 1963).

21. Franz Fanon *Wretched of the Earth* (New York: Grore Press, 1965).

22. *Ibid.*, pp. 98–108.

23. Ann Douglas, *The Feminization of American Culture* (New York: Knopf, 1977), p. 53.

24. *Ibid.*

25. For a historical study of this period, with special attention to the experience of women in the early factories, see Hannah Josephson, *Golden Threads: New England Millgirls and Magnates* (New York: Russell 1967). For a view of the money that made the mills, see Russell Adams, Jr., *The Boston Money Tree* (New York: Crowell, 1977).

26. Douglas, chap. 4, "The Loss of Theology: From Dogma to Fiction," pp. 121–164.
27. For a discussion of feminist women in this period see Carroll Smith-Rosenberg, "Beauty, the Beast, and the Militant Woman," *American Quarterly*, 23 (1971), 576–583; see also the previously cited Douglas book and Nancy F. Cott, *The Bonds of Womanhood: "Woman's Sphere" in New England, 1780–1835* (New Haven, Conn.: Yale University Press, 1977).
28. Cott, p. 206.

TWO: UNDERSTANDING RELATIONSHIPS

1. Georg Simmel, *The Sociology of Georg Simmel,* translated and edited by Kurt Wolff (New York: Free Press, 1964), p. 118.
2. *Ibid.,* p. 135.
3. *Ibid.,* p. 136.
4. On the stranger see *ibid.,* pp. 402–408. For discussions of the formal properties of groups see the sociological journal *Sociometry.*
5. On nonverbal communication see Edward T. Hall, *The Silent Language* (Garden City, N.Y.: Doubleday, 1959), and the popular literature on body language, but do not take the latter too seriously. For a more scientific analysis of nonverbal communication see Ray Birdwhistell, *Kinesics and Context: Essays on Body Motion Communication* (Philadelphia: University of Pennsylvania Press, 1970).
6. See Freed Bales, *Interaction Process Analysis* (Chicago: University of Chicago Press, 1951). This is the original study in this area. For a summary of work in group-interaction research, see Theodore Mills, *Sociology of Small Groups* (Englewood Cliffs, N.J.: Prentice-Hall, 1970).
7. Constantin Stanislavski, *Creating a Role,* translated by Elizabeth R. Hapgood (New York: Theater Arts Books, 1961).
8. This line is from *As You Like It.*
9. For a discussion of the conference by an observer who was not a participant, see Norman Birnbaum, *Toward a Critical Sociology* (New York: Oxford University Press, 1971).
10. Erving Goffman, *The Presentation of Self in Everyday Life* (Garden City N.Y.: Doubleday, 1959).
11. Scott Turow, *One L.* (Baltimore: Penguin, 1977), p. 126.
12. For a discussion of the sociology of Max Weber see Reinhard Bendix, *Max Weber: An Intellectual Portrait* (Garden City, N.Y.: Doubleday, 1960).
13. Stanley Milgram, *Obedience to Authority* (New York: Harper & Row, 1975).
14. *Ibid.,* p. 188.
15. *Ibid.,* p. 122.
16. *Ibid.,* p. 174.
17. Interview on CBS by Roger Mudd, reprinted in *ibid.,* p. 185.
18. Other experimenters have worked on group pressure. The early work of Solomon Asch is especially recommended.

19. Philippe Aries, *Centuries of Childhood: A Social History of Family Life*, translated by Robert Baldick (New York: Vintage Books, 1963, p. 128.

20. For a discussion of the influence early colonial living conditions had on education see Lawrence A. Cremin, *American Education: The Colonial Experience 1607–1783* (New York: Harper & Row, 1970).

21. Joseph F. Kett, *Rites of Passage: Adolescence in America, 1790 to the Present* (New York: Basic Books, 1977), p. 216.

22. For a discussion of this point see Samuel Eliot Morison, *Harvard College in the Seventeenth Century* (Cambridge, Mass.: Harvard University Press, 1936).

23. Kett, p. 23.

24. *Ibid.*, p.

25. David Hackett Fischer, *Growing Old in America* (New York: Oxford University Press, 1977), p. 4.

26. *Ibid.*, p. 26–76.

27. *Ibid.*, p. 92. See also Bernard Bailyn, *Ideological Origins of the American Revolution* (Cambridge, Mass.: Harvard University Press, 1967).

28. The 1960s saw the most recent example of age power, the organized push by the old to get the Medicare legislation enacted. For an objective description, see Richard Harris, *A Sacred Trust* (New York: New American Library, 1966).

THREE: FINDING WORK

1. For a discussion of the ways in which work was assigned in the Middle Ages based on accident of birth, see Walter Ullmann, *Individual and Society in the Middle Ages* (Baltimore: Johns Hopkins University Press, 1966).

2. Emile Durkheim, *The Division of Labor in Society* (Glencoe, Ill.: Free Press, 1947).

3. This really happened, about ten years ago, and was reported in the *New York Times*. I have *not* been able to find the article.

4. For a recent review of the problems relating education to work, see HEW, *Work in America* (Cambridge: M.I.T. Press, 1973).

5. Aaron V. Cicourel and John I. Kitsuse, *The Educational Decision-Makers* (Indianapolis, Ind.: Bobbs-Merrill, 1963).

6. Christopher Jencks and David Riesman, *The Academic Revolution* (Chicago: University of Chicago Press, 1977).

7. Everett C. Hughes, *Men and Their Work* (New York: Free Press, 1958), p. 40–41.

8. Howard S. Becker, Blanche Geer, Everett C. Hughes, and Anselm Strauss, *Boys in White* (Chicago: University of Chicago Press, 1961).

9. *Ibid.*, p. 111.

10. Howard S. Becker and Blanche Geer, "The Fate of Idealism in Medical School," *American Sociological Review*, 23 (February 1958), 50–56.

11. Blanche Geer ed., *Learning to Work* (Los Angeles: Sage Publications, 1974).

12. *Ibid.*
13. For an extended discussion of the role of occupational groups as political action groups see Elliott A. Krause, *The Sociology of Occupations* (Boston: Little, Brown, 1971).
14. See *ibid.*, concluding chapter, "The Politics of Skill."
15. Marsha Millman, *The Unkindest Cut* (New York: Morrow, 1977).
16. *Ibid.*, p. 145.
17. See three related books by Elliot Freidson on this subject: *Profession of Medicine* (New York: Dodd, Mead, 1970), *Professional Dominance* (New York: Atherton, 1970), and *Doctoring Together* (New York: Elsevier, 1976).
18. As an example of a study by activist political socialists, see for example, Joseph Page and Mary-Win O'Brien, *Bitter Wages. Ralph Nader's Study Group Report on Occupational Health.* (New York, Grossman, 1973).
19. For a discussion of this key transitional period see Charles A. Beard, *Economic Interpretation of the American Constitution* (Glencoe, Ill.: Free Press, 1935).
20. A critical school of historians is now revising the literature of the past in the light of fuller statistical evidence and without the conservative political bias that characterized much past history writing. See, as an example of a study on the old South, Eugene Genovese, *Roll, Jordan, Roll: The World the Slave-Holders Made* (New York: Pantheon, 1969).
21. On this dimension in American political indoctrination, which often poses as neutral information provision, see Samuel Bowles and Herbert Gintis, *Schooling in Capitalist America* (New York: Basic Books, 1975). Almost a century earlier Emile Durkheim was much concerned with the role of values in education and encouraged just such indoctrination.
22. Raoul Berger, a legal scholar of great repute, suggests that the government, especially the Supreme Court, may be exceeding the strict limit of the Constitution in acting in this manner. See his recent book, *Government by Judiciary* (Cambridge, Mass.: Harvard University Press, 1977). On the other hand, from Frankfurter to Douglas, some justices have noted the probusiness bias of the court.
23. For an important interpretation of the reasons for the westward migration see Charles Beard, *Economic Interpretation of the American Constitution* (New York: Macmillan, 1935).
24. Stephan Thernstrom, *Poverty and Progress: Social Mobility in a Nineteenth Century City* (Cambridge, Mass.: Harvard University Press, 1964).
25. *Ibid.*, pp. 138–165.
26. See, for the Fifties, C. Wright Mills, *The Power Elite* (New York, Oxford University Press, 1936, and see his collected essays, *Power, Politics and People.* (New York, Oxford Univ. Press, 1963.) For a more recent discussion see G. William Domhoff, *The Higher Circles: The Governing Class in America.* (New York, Random House, 1971) But see Chap. 5 of this book, for both Mills and Domhoff tend to oversimplify the problem.
27. Christopher Jencks, Marshall Smith, Henry Ackland, Mary Jo Bane, David Cohen, Herbert Gintis, Barbara Heyns, and Stephen Michelson,

Inequality: A Reassessment of the Effect of Family and Schooling in America (New York: Harper & Row, 1973).

28. Mark S. Granovetter, *Getting a Job: A Study of Contacts and Careers* (Cambridge, Mass.: Harvard University Press, 1974).

29. On this lawyer illustration compare these two books: Erwin Smigel, *Wall Street Lawyer*, and Jerome E. Carlin, *Lawyers on their Own: A Study of Individual Practitioners in Chicago* (New Brunswick, N.J.: Rutgers University Press, 1962).

30. Economists call this phenomenon the dual labor market. Much recent work at the U.S. Labor Department in Washington tends to substantiate that it exists.

31. Louise Kapp Howe, *Pink Collar Workers* (New York: Avon, 1977).

32. *Ibid.*, p. 78.

33. *Ibid.*, Appendix M.

34. Edward Gross, "Plus a change? The Sexual Structure of Occupations Over Time," *Social Problems*, 16 (Fall 1968), 198–208.

35. *Ibid.*, p. 208.

36. Some women's action groups have had financial problems staying alive. Some, such as the Boston Women's Health Collective have managed to continue through the sales of books written by members. See Boston Women's Health Book Collective, *Our Bodies, Ourselves* (New York: Simon and Schuster, 1976), and their follow-up, Boston Women's Health Collective, *Ourselves and Our Children: A Book By and For Parents* (New York: Random House, 1978).

37. Betty Friedan, *The Feminine Mystique* (New York: Norton, 1963).

38. Rosabeth Moss Kanter, *Men and Women of the Corporation* (New York: Basic Books, 1977).

39. Mary Roth Walsh, *Doctors Wanted: No Women Need Apply* (New Haven, Conn.: Yale University Press, 1977).

40. The job shortage in academia and the continuing overproduction of Ph.D.s, is intensifying the problems of women there.

41. Nathan Glazer, *Affirmative Discrimination: Ethnic Equality and Public Policy* (New York: Basic Books, 1976).

42. Max Weber, "Bureaucracy," in H. H. Gerth and C. Wright Mills (eds. and translators), *From Max Weber: Essays in Sociology* (New York: Oxford University Press, 1946).

43. For an excellent discussion of Weber's political sociology see Reinhard Bendix, *Max Weber: An Intellectual Portrait* (Garden City, N.Y.: Doubleday, 1960).

44. William H. Whyte, *The Organization Man* (New York: Simon and Schuster, 1956).

45. Michel Crozier, *The Bureaucratic Phenomenon* (Chicago: Univ. of Chicago Press, 1964), pp. 89–139.

46. Kanter.

47. Whyte did not have historical data here.

48. *Ibid.*, p. 184.

49. *Ibid.*, pp. 184–185.

50. This situation was discussed by Andre Gorz in *Strategy for Labor* (Boston: Beacon Press), 1967.
51. Erving Goffman, *Asylums*. See p. 34 in this book.
52. Kanter, *Ibid.*
53. Rosabeth Moss Kanter, *Committment and Community* (Cambridge: Harvard Univ. Press, 1972).

FOUR: JOINING A COMMUNITY

1. Carl Sandburg, "Chicago," *Complete Poems* (New York: Harcourt, Brace, 1950), p. 3.
2. Sandburg, "The Windy City," *ibid.*, p. 279.
3. *Ibid.*, p. 277.
4. See especially Robert E. Faris, *Chicago Sociology* 1920–1932. (Chicago: University of Chicago Press, 1970).
5. For a discussion by Park see Robert E. Park, and Ernest W. Burgess, *City*. Morris Janowitz, ed. (Chicago: University of Chicago Press, 1967.)
6. Robert Park, "The City: Suggestions for the Investigation of Human Behavior in the City Enviornment," *American Journal of Sociology*, 20 (March 1915), 577–612.
7. *Ibid.*, 581.
8. *Ibid.*, 581, 584.
9. *Ibid.*, 594.
10. *Ibid.*, 595.
11. *Ibid.*, 603.
12. *Ibid.*, 604.
13. William Foote Whyte, *Street Corner Society* (Chicago: University of Chicago Press, 1943).
14. William Foote Whyte, "The Slum: On the Evolution of Street Corner Society," in Arthur J. Vidich, Joseph Bensman, and Maurice R. Stein (eds.), *Reflections on Community Studies* (New York: Wiley, 1964), p. 19.
15. *Ibid.*, p. 19.
16. Whyte, *Street Corner Society*, pp. 23–25.
17. *Ibid.*, pp. 111–146.
18. *Ibid.*, p. 240.
19. Whyte, "Slum," p. 69.
20. Kevin Lynch, *The Image of the City* (Cambridge, Mass.: M.I.T. Press, 1960), pp. 46–90.
21. This was reported in *New York* magazine in late 1976. The technique used was essentially that of Lynch.
22. Eliot Liebow, *Tally's Corner* (Boston: Little, Brown, 1967), pp. 161–207.
23. Herbert Gans, *The Urban Villagers: Group and Class in the Life of Italian-Americans* (New York: Free Press, 1962), pp. 229–262.
24. Marc Fried, *The World of the Urban Working Class* (Cambridge, Mass.: Harvard University Press, 1973).
25. Gans, p. 290.
26. Nathan Glazer and Daniel P. Moynihan, *Beyond the Melting Pot* The

Negroes, *Puerto Ricans, Jews, Italians, and Irish of New York City* (Cambridge, Mass.: M.I.T. Press), 1970

27. Herbert J. Gans, *The Levittowners: Ways of Life and Politics in a New Suburban Community* (New York: Random House, 1967), pp. 173–174.
28. *Ibid.*, pp. 97–98.
29. John R. Seeley, R. Alexander Sim, and Elizabeth W. Loosely, *Crestwood Heights: A Study of the Culture of Suburban Life* (New York: Wiley, 1963).
30. *Ibid.*, pp. 42–62.
31. Maurice Stein and Arthur J. Vidich, *Small Town in Mass Society* (Princeton, N.J.: Princeton University Press, 1968).
32. Arthur J. Vidich and Joseph Bensman, "The Springdale Case: Academic Bureaucrats and Townspeople," in Vidich, Bensman and Stein, (eds.,) pp. 319–323.
33. *Ibid.*, p. 342.
34. Gloria Aull, interviewed in Steward Dill McBride, "They Fought a Highway and Formed a Congress," *Christian Science Monitor,* September 9, 1977, p. 18.
35. *Ibid.*
36. *Ibid.*
37. Steward Dill McBride, "How a Community Won a Redlining Battle," *Christian Science Monitor,* Octorber 14, 1977, p. 19–20. It should be noted that the stabilized and improving neighborhood is now 85 percent black.
38. Introduction to series *"A Nation of Neighborhoods,"* *Christian Science Monitor,* September 9, 1977.

FIVE: ACTING POLITICALLY

1. See, for example, the records and studies collected about the activities, at Williams College, Williamstown, Mass.
2. Of course it took far less than thirty years to experience the three eras named for these decades. 'Fifties-style" culture and politics lasted till about 1962, and those of the seventies began about 1972.
3. Kent Jennings and Richard Niemi, *The Political Character of Adolescence* (Princeton, N.J.: Princeton University Press, 1977), p. 329.
4. *Ibid.*
5. For discussions of this problem read *TV Guide* regularly. Serious issues are brought up here.
6. The transition from subject to citizen is beautifully summarized in Walter Ullmann, *Individual and Society in the Middle Ages.* (Baltimore: Johns Hopkins University Press, 1966.)
7. For a discussion of this see the classic by Charles A. Beard, *An Economic Interpretation of the American Constitution* (Glencoe, Ill.: Free Press, 1935).
8. Robert R. Alford and Roger Friedland, "Political Participation and Public Policy," *Annual Review of Sociology,* 1 (1975), 430.
9. *Ibid.*, 443.
10. Sidney Verba and N. H. Nie, *Participation in America: Political Democracy and Social Equality* (New York: Harper & Row, 1972).

11. Lester W. Milbrath, *Political Participation: How and Why Do People Get Involved in Politics?* (Chicago: Rand McNally, 1965).

12. Elliott A. Krause, "Functions of a Bureaucratic Ideology: Citizen Participation," *Social Problems,* 16 (1968), 129–143.

13. Frances Fox Piven and Richard Cloward, *Poor People's Movements: How They Succeed, Why They Fail* (New York: Basic Books, 1977), p. 36.

14. Robert and Helen Lynd, *Middletown in transition* (New York: Harcourt, Brace, 1937).

15. Floyd Hunter, *Community Power Structure* (Garden City, N.Y.: Doubleday, 1963).

16. Robert Dahl, *Who Governs?* (New Haven, Conn.: Yale University Press, 1964).

17. George Orwell, *Animal Farm* (New York: Harcourt, Brace, 1954).

18. Raymond Vernon *Metropolis 1985: An Interpretation of the Findings of the New York Metropolitan Region Study* (Cambridge.: Harvard Univ. Press 1960.)

19. See the biography by Mike Royko, *Boss* (New York: NAL, 1971).

20. Robert A. Caro, *The Power Broker: Robert Moses and the Fall of New York* (New York: Knopf, 1974), pp. 17–18.

21. See V. I. Lenin, *The State and Revolution* (New York: International, 1932).

22. For examples of modern Marxian theory see Nicos Poulantzas, *Political Power and Social Classes* (London: New Left Books, 1974), and Ralph Miliband, *Marxism and Politics* (New York: Oxford University Press, 1977).

23. For a recent assessment of the consumer movement, see Howe, *Ibid.*

24. This is very important. Capitalism is an impersonal system that must work this way. Many individual capitalists are well-meaning, socially liberal individuals, but the system is not socially liberal and cannot act this way. At least that's my opinion.

SIX: THINKING SOCIOLOGICALLY

1. Robert K. Merton, "Anomie, Anomia, and Social Interaction: Contexts of Deviant Behavior," in Marshall Clinard (ed.,) *Anomie and Deviant Behavior* (New York: Free Press, 1964), p. 215.

2. Merton, p. 216.

3. Howard S. Becker, *Outsiders. Studies in the Sociology of Deviance* (London: Collier-MacMillan, 1963), pp. 41–78.

4. The central work by Emile Durkheim on this subject is his *Suicide*

5. For a discussion of Max Weber's ideas see Raymond Aron, *Main Currents in Sociological Thought,* vol. II, *Durkheim, Pareto, and Weber* (Garden City, N.Y.: Doubleday, 1970). This also contains an excellent discussion of Durkheim's ideas.

Index of Sociological Concepts
and Authors

Index of Sociological Concepts and Authors

About The Author

Elliot Krause was born in Cleveland, Ohio in 1936. He was graduated from Harvard College in 1958 and received his M.A. and Ph.D. in sociology from Boston University in 1962 and 1966, respectively. He has been research consultant to the Massachusetts Department of Mental Health, the Office of Economic Opportunity, HEW's Committee on Work in America, and the Office of the Secretary of HEW. He is the author of numerous articles in the sociology of occupations, political sociology, and the sociology of health in American, French Canadian, and French publications and is the author of *The Sociology of Occupations* (1971) and *Power and Illness: The Political Sociology of Health and Medical Care* (1977). He is presently professor of sociology at Northeastern University.